For Steve Johnsen - the good
times we've shared fishing in the
past and the good times yet to come.
Happy Thanksgiving 1996!
Best wishes,
George Reiger

West of Key West

West of Key West

edited by John Cole and Hawk Pollard

paintings by Peter Corbin

sidebar paintings by David Harrison Wright

STACKPOLE
BOOKS

Published by
STACKPOLE BOOKS
5067 Ritter Road
Mechanicsburg, PA 17055

Printed in Hong Kong

10   9   8   7   6   5   4   3   2   1

First edition

Photographs by Jeffrey Cardenas and Gil Drake

Library of Congress Cataloging-in-Publication Data
West of Key West / edited and compiled by John Cole.
      p.   cm.
    ISBN 0-8117-1881-6 (hc)
    1. Saltwater fly fishing—Florida—Key West—Anecdotes. I.
Cole, John N., 1923–   .
SH456.2.W47   1996
799.1'6634—dc20   95-52458
                                                              CIP

"AIRBORNE" *frontispiece by John Rice*

CONTENTS

GIL DRAKE

GIL DRAKE

ACKNOWLEDGMENTS

MANY THANKS TO JEAN AND JOHN COLE; Dick Florschutz, my Marquesas partner; and Harlan Franklin, who continues to put up with my lousy casting. Much appreciation also to Guy de la Valdéne, who, while he probably won't remember it, was instrumental in arranging my first trip to the flats west of Key West; to Tiger Thouron, with whom I ventured forth; and to the ascetic Gil Drake, whose fish-finding powers have astounded far better anglers than I.

All those named got me going, kept me going, and, finally, brought me to the point where I felt we should create something to fix in time this extraordinary, unequaled, and fragile ecosystem that we are allowed, for the moment, to enjoy—the boundless flats of the Key West National Wildlife Refuge.

Finally, I lift my glass to the writers, artists, and photographers whose work appears herein. It has been my privilege to associate with you all.

—*Hawk Pollard*

Introduction

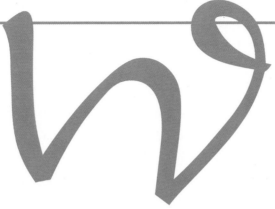

HEN WRITERS AS GOOD AS THE CONTRIBUTORS to this book can each write so well about a single, small place on our planet, that place must be exceptional.

Which is true. Travel from the Content Keys northwest of Big Pine Key west to Sawyer Key and Riding Key and on to the Snipe Keys, the Mud Keys, and past Calda Bank across Northwest Channel to Archer Key, Barracouta Key, Man Key, Woman Key, Boca Grande, and across Boca Grande Channel to the Marquesas and you will discover the place itself. But you will not know it any more than Captain John Smith knew North America when he came ashore at Jamestown.

For these waters that embrace the Lower Keys—the Atlantic on the south and the Gulf of Mexico on the north—are some of the most intricate in the world. Channels embroider each of the small, marly islands that curve in a tenuous necklace from Marathon to Key West.

You can see them, and cross some of them, as you drive over the many bridges of the Overseas Highway. But you can not comprehend their complexity until you travel by boat. Which, of necessity, will have to be a small boat because so much of this water is so shallow.

"Thin water" it's called, but the phrase is misleading. Yes, there are scores of square miles of flats where the water is less than two feet deep. But this unique environment pulses with life. It is rich, not thin; mysterious, not thin; breathtaking, not thin. It is shoal, but there are depths of wonder that you will find nowhere else.

And discovering those wonders will likely get you lost. It is then that you will begin to know something of the extraordinary adventures this place can make possible. For then you will comprehend just how vast this relatively small place can be.

These keys, these mangrove hummocks, these shallows, these flats, these winding threads and ribbons of channels, these astonishing intricacies of interlaced land, water, sponge, coral, powder-soft sand, mud, and marl are as complex as curving Arabic etchings scrolled on the side of a silver flask. Try to follow each hair-thin line and you end where you began, unsure of where you have been.

There are countless places on these thin waters, places no larger than a cornfield, where an angler-explorer can spend a year or two and still be surprised by fresh discoveries. The seasons change, the tides change, water temperatures rise and fall, winds blow from around the compass, or do not blow at all. And each time any one of these shifts in the smallest increments, the creatures that travel and live in these thin waters alter their schedules, change their habits, move from here to there, in and out of your ken. There is no end to the mysteries that abound, no end whatsoever. You can search a lifetime, but you will not return to the precise place where you began. These flats, this place, these thin waters from the Contents to the Marquesas have more secrets than the ocean deep.

Which is why so many of the nation's finest writers and best artists and accomplished anglers can find so much that is particular and individual to tell us about. There is so much out there.

Which is why there is such variety in the pages of this book: The environment portrayed on those pages is diverse beyond imagining.

Which is why you will find fiction and nonfiction written by recognized and distinguished authors. And why you will read accounts by the highly professional guides who explore these waters anew each day. And why there are stories by anglers like you, come to these waters only occasionally, but discovering in each occasion those moments they will never forget.

Just as the writers find their own originality in the uniqueness of the flats experience, so do different artists record varying views of the same flats and their creatures. For these places are alive, and because they live, they are forever in motion, evolving before the artist's eyes. What are caught in their paintings are parts of moments that together make up an impression of the whole.

This book brings you a kind of flats kaleidoscope. It identifies many of the creatures who live above and below the water's shimmering surface. It empowers you to see this world through the eyes of others. The people who wrote the stories, the artists who painted the paintings, and the photographers who took the photographs . . . all of them hope that as you read and look through this book you will begin to understand why the place each of them portrays is such a true mystery, such a fine exception, and of such extraordinary and fragile diversity.

GIL DRAKE

When you have read this book, you will know more about fishing, even if you think you already know a great deal. And, more importantly, you will be more aware of the wonders of these waters, which, in turn, should commit you to the acts and ideas that are necessary to protect and save this remarkable marine environment for anglers and explorers yet unborn.

—*John Cole*

RIGHT TIME, RIGHT PLACE

Peter Kaminsky

TARPON IS A BIG FISH, BIG AS A PERSON, BIG AS A DEER. Nothing you can take on light tackle offers such a challenging fight. To stalk and hook one in shallow water on a bone white flat requires the intense focus of still hunting. The reward is one-on-one combat with a leaping, head-shaking, tail-walking opponent who has a whole ocean's worth of running room. If some sadistic judge said that he would empty my memory banks of all but one fishing memory, the one I would keep would be that of a big tarpon who was grazing on some Gulf shrimp when I intruded upon him one hot June morning in the Florida Keys.

The day before, my wife, Melinda, and I parked our daughters with my folks at the family's ancestral condo in West Palm and headed south, stopping, as we always do, for some fried grouper with tamarind hot sauce and a slice of key lime pie at Manny & Isa's in Islamorada.

If I had been sleeping that dawn in Key West, the alarm would have awakened me at four-fifteen. What I'd been doing was staring at the sky, thinking about fish. It's something I'll never shake the first night of a trip. Jean had left three box lunches on the table (two for Melinda and me and one for our guide, David Kesar). We crossed the street, went down to the dock, and Dave and his skiff glided in.

We moved out of Key West Harbor at idle speed, skirting Christmas Tree and Tank islands. Still in darkness, Dave picked up speed and set our course for a faint star hanging low on the horizon. The star stayed low as we neared it. It wasn't a star: it was a marker buoy. Then an eight-mile run, picking our way by the reflectors of lobster pot markers that Dave located by shining his searchlight.

We flew through the darkness. Still in the lee of Key West, the water was calm. Next we crossed Boca Grande Channel, the same channel, Dave observed, that the tarpon stream through on their way up the west coast of Florida. We had wind against tide. The chop got heavier. The eastern sky lightened. Dave drove, baseball cap on backwards for reasons of practicality, not style.

The sun rose as we reached the Marquesas, a circle of hummocks sitting at the entry to the Gulf. The water took on its dawn colors—a stained glass window of robin's egg blue frosted with the gray sheen of low light and shot through with sun-up's flame pink.

Dave cut the engine and the boat settled down off the plane. A porpoise leaped in front of us, blotting out the sun and reflecting it back a thousand times in the spray of drops that she threw off as she rose in the air. No doubt our engine had attracted her. There's something about the sound that says, "Come here and play."

I know this for a fact because some years ago I worked on a film about dolphin out on the Bahamas Bank, a desolate piece of nowhere on the edge of the Gulf Stream. Some salvagers who worked on the wreck of a Peruvian treasure galleon discovered that whenever they ran their outboards, dolphins would come and leap and circle and generally want to play with the crew. According to Steve Leatherwood, a noted dolphin specialist on our film crew, it was the only game in town, and the dolphins flocked to it the way a shiny sports car in a high school parking lot will attract a flock of teenage boys. At any rate, with none of this foreknowledge, we brought our best *Close Encounters*-type dolphin-attracting music: We tried recordings of dolphins' love bleeps and whistles. From the so-called universal language of music, we selected Beethoven, Chuck Berry, Kenny G., reaching out, species to species. It was real New Age, crystal-gazing kind of stuff, but the dolphins could not have cared less until we fired up our Evinrudes and then, without fail, they came.

"THE BATTLE IS ENGAGED" *Peter Corbin*

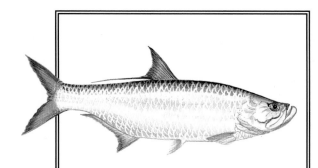

TARPON

Megalops atlantica

Although the name silver king has been overworked in angling prose, the tarpon does, in fact, deserve its royalty. Few dramas on the flats equal the knee-knocking majesty of a school of tarpon as the huge, violet torpedoes glide toward your skiff, their dark shadows rippling like serpents across the pale shoals.

In the Marquesas, however, we were looking for tarpon, not dolphin. Dave got up on his poling platform and we moved across the flat, no sounds, no wake. Dave spoke sotto voce, "If you look at two o'clock, you'll see two fins. Sharks. They're mating."

We looked. I'd never given it much thought, but even sharks have to take time out from their busy schedules as marauding predators in order to make baby sharks. We gave them a wide berth and moved around the island, entering a broad lagoon. There was a light breeze, and the sun was high enough to light up the whole flat.

Spotting bonefish takes some getting used to. Likewise, permit. But a hundred-pound tarpon, its sides flashing as it feeds, announces itself with authority. A feeding pod cruised in front of us.

"Strip about sixty feet of line," Dave said. "When the tarpon lines up with the fly, cast. Lead him by six feet."

I stood. Dave poled. We followed the tarpon. Dave tried to flank them and come around so I would have a clear right-handed cast.

"Now," he said.

I gave one false cast, opened up, and double-hauled, hard. The fly, a Marquesa Sunrise Special with a narrow, delicate profile, sank in the clear water like a maple leaf from a tree on a windless Indian summer day. The tarpon changed course, ever so slightly. He had seen the fly. I began to strip. The tarpon inhaled the streamer.

"Keep stripping until the line tightens. The tarpon has a mouth that can hold gallons of water. It takes some time for the fly to find flesh. When you feel him, slam him really hard as many times as you can. When he breaks water, bow."

Bowing to the tarpon is a two-step maneuver where you extend your arms and drop your rod tip, thereby ensuring that the airborne weight of the fish does not bear down fully on the tippet. Otherwise, a hundred-pound fish will part a twenty-pound leader every time. The tarpon broke water, sailing into the air. For some reason, I was reminded of the first time my parents took me to a drive-in movie. I think the feature was *Alice in Wonderland.* The images on the screen seemed fantastically large. I'd been to the movies before, but only in a darkened theater. Seen against the scale of a parking lot full of two-ton cars, I was thrilled at the sight of "shrunken" Alice looming over the huge American cars and topping the tallest trees.

The tarpon was like that. As he rocketed into the air, he looked like a billboard-sized photo enlargement of a fish. I bowed. "Good job," Dave said. The tarpon crashed back into the water. I reared back and slammed him again, and again, and again. For the next half hour I recovered line and the tarpon wrenched it back, jumping a score of times. The trick to tarpon fishing, Dave told me, is to dominate quickly. This fish was not about to be dominated, at least not by me.

I went from the bow to the stern completing circuit after circuit of Dave's sixteen-foot Maverick Mirage. The fish was ten yards away. He leaped. The line slipped through the guides. I began the exercise over again. We moved like two dancers having a body language debate over who is going to lead. About a hundred yards out, where my line met the water, there was a series of violent splashes. I thought we had entered a new stage of the fight, the tarpon having lost the strength to jump. Not so. A shark tore into the tarpon. The water frothed. It didn't last more than fifteen seconds. The line went slack. Oh well, I had hooked the first tarpon I had cast to and he gave me the fight of my life.

We poled the flat for an hour. There were tarpon, but they stayed out of range. The summer sun began to wilt us. We returned to Key West, arriving about noon, and headed for our lodgings. A breeze coming off the harbor and the hum of the ceiling fan in my bedroom sent me right to sleep.

Three hours later I had a craving for some Cuban food, so Melinda and I walked into town. An obliging policewoman sent us to El Meson de Pepe on the southern end of the island. It was pleasantly dark and cold inside, made more dark by the contrast of the brilliant scene outside the window. We were the only diners. I drank two cold beers and dug into a plate of shrimp with garlic, a dozen stone crabs, and a helping of ropa vieja—old rope—so called because it is based on a cut of beef that is cooked until the flesh unravels just like an old shirt that's been through the wash too many times. The waitresses kept up a lively discussion on the relative merits of different hair care products.

At four-thirty, John, my afternoon angler-guest, and I met Dave at the dock. We moved just outside the harbor and set two anchors (fore and aft) in the racing tidal current. We were hoping to catch the "worm hatch" that Dave reported had come on strong the previous evening, driving the tarpon mad. The worm, a little red squiggle known by its Spanish name, *palolo,* inhabits the crannies of the coral bedrock and molts every June at the peak of the tarpon run, when millions of tarpon are streaming north out of the Rio Colorado and The Parasiminas, past Chetumal Bay, coastwise in the shadow of the pyramid of Tulum: a great annual migration to summer feeding grounds that reach from Galveston, around the Keys and then north, paralleling the Gulf Stream past Montauk where they are reported to have been taken on rod and reel by puzzled striper fisherman. At just that moment when tarpon are pouring into the Gulf, the palolos hatch out of the coral bedrock of the Keys.

John, David, and I sat in the boat . . . waiting for the worms. I kept peering down into the racing current. In the space of five minutes, the water filled with worms. A tarpon rolled, then another, and another. The surface of the Gulf looked like the Beaverkill at the peak of the Hendriksen hatch, or more aptly, the Sulphur hatch, when the trout take emerging nymphs just under the surface, splashing and rolling. It was intense, only the fish were a hundred times larger than trout.

I cast and stripped, cast and stripped, getting into the rhythm. It crossed my mind that my little artificial might go unnoticed by the feeding fish, but I kept casting. After ten minutes John took a turn and then Dave. The rod came around to me again. I cast and talked. Dave remarked on a nice boat that was going by. I turned my head to look back, leaving my fly hanging in the current. That was the time, of course, that the tarpon chose to slam it. I reacted. The tarpon took air and broke off.

"Hmm," John said, which in a Downeaster passes for hysterical excitement. (John is a Maine transplant.)

I rose to the bait. "Hmm what, John?" I asked.

"The tarpon took your fly at the end of the swing, just the way a salmon will roll and take. I think if we treat this current like a salmon stream, and fish it that way, we might be on to something. Anyway, it couldn't hurt."

I gave John the rod. He cast across the current, quartering down tide. "Right . . . about . . . there," John said more to himself than to us. "Whomp, tarpon on." The fish jumped and broke off. Dave tried. I tried. We hooked a dozen fish, one of them within ten feet of the boat. When he took to the air he sprayed us like a Labrador shaking the water off his wet coat.

We didn't land any fish. This was much different from the comparatively Zen exercise of fighting a fish on the flats when you let the tarpon run as long and as far as he wants, like trout or a salmon in a big pool. In contrast, the evening's fish were hanging at the edge of a fast and powerful current. They took the fly with a punch and they shook with equal force. It was up close, physical fishing. I imagined I could hear the tarpon cursing our mothers as they broke off. It was glorious, furious action, and John wore the blissed-out smile of an angler who has figured it out for a particular time and place.

The hatch slowed. The tarpon stopped. I had been watching the progress of a water spout bearing down on Fleming Key, its funnel cloud writhing like a swaying cobra. We turned for home.

THE FASCINATION OF WHAT'S DIFFICULT

Dan Gerber

THERE IS A POSSIBILITY OF GOING CRAZY OUT HERE ON THIS glassy water on a falling tide. And going slightly crazy is part of the idea, crazy in the sense of getting lost in it and, more to the point, of losing ourselves. To the ways in which normal people think, we would have to be a little crazy to devote so much energy and so many precious hours of our lives to trying to fool one particular kind of soft-lipped fish into believing a quarter-sized dollop of beige yarn and feathers with a couple of beady lead eyes, giving it the aghast expression of a thyroid patient, might be the succulent crab that it's been seeking for lunch.

We are poling a broad flat on the west side of the Marquesas, zeroing in on a little patch of nervous water where, a moment ago, we are almost certain we saw the brief silver flash of a tailing permit. We know however, from long experience, that what caught our attention may have simply been our desire to see a permit's tail pierce the surface like a filleting knife as the elusive fish angles down to the shallow bottom to eat something about the size and shape of the fly I'm holding between the thumb and forefinger of my casting hand.

Fly fishing on the flats from a small skiff is really a team sport. You can do it alone if you have enough skill and patience, but since you're trying to spot and hunt down an individual fish without letting him know you're there, the results are seldom satisfying. Especially for permit. It usually takes an experienced set of eyes to discern

the shape and movement of your quarry through moving water against the highly variegated bottom of coral heads, sponges, sand, and turtle grass from a platform arched above the outboard motor, and a fine sense of geometry to pole the boat close enough in an attitude toward the fish where the angler, standing ready on the bow with ninety or a hundred feet of line stripped out, can present his fly to the fish without spooking it and without snagging the poler off his perch on the backcast.

I had been at this game six years without success. In that time I boated and released a few magnificent tarpon and a few dozen barracuda on flies and took a couple of spectacular permit on a spinning rod with live crabs. But fooling a permit with a fly is another matter. Taking a permit on a crab is a fine thing to do, like getting your bat on a good high-school fastball, but taking one on a fly is a real feat, akin to making at least a blooper single off Nolan Ryan. In those six years I'd had maybe three dozen opportunities to put a permit on the other end of my fly line. A few of those I blew with sloppy casting and a dozen more spooked before my guide and longtime coconspirator, Simon Becker, could pole the boat close enough to give me the opportunity of scaring them off with great fat loops of white fly line waved over their heads like a semaphore of impending doom. But there were a dozen times, at least, when my imitation crab, for some perverse reason called a Merkin, had settled down perfectly in front of a feeding permit and been twitched with the subtlest little strips of line, only to have this most finicky of the family Carangidae brush it aside with its severely snubbed snout and turn away haughtily as if its intelligence had been insulted, or maybe even its morals.

In spite of their name, permit are not the kind of girls you meet at the bar and wake up with in the morning. They're the kind you court with flowers, jewels, dinners in expensive restaurants, and proposals of marriage, a once- or maybe twice-in-

"FLORIDA PERMIT" *Peter Corbin*

a-lifetime kind of love. There are many highly accomplished saltwater fly fishermen who haven't had the pleasure of battling a permit, though there are a few obsessive types who have made a career of pursuing permit and, in an extreme case, like Del Brown who spends upwards of a hundred days a year at it, have enticed several hundred to take a fly. And there are places in the Caribbean and in the shoal waters of Mexico where, so my more widely experienced fishing friends tell me, permit are generally smaller and a good bit more silly than they are on the flats off the Florida Keys. There are also anglers who have claimed permit on flies offshore after bringing them to a feeding frenzy with chum, but that's a whole other order of experience, more like shooting a captive kudu on a game ranch and offering the trophy as evidence that one is a skillful hunter.

Fly fishing for permit is the fortuitous coming together of a broad range of long-practiced skills to locate, stalk, mystify, out fence, capture, and safely release an idea clothed in intelligence, weariness, tenacity, and fins. It requires a knowledge of tides, currents, winds, temperature, and the behavior of birds and rays, vigilance, instinct, muscular and delicate casting, maybe out to ninety feet in a bothering wind, timing and sensitivity in setting the hook, a lot of luck in clearing the line to the reel, and from there on, the strength of your arms, understanding of the fish, dexterity, readiness of wit and, if it all works out, the grace not to gloat about it. It's really more akin to hunting than to trolling for dolphin, reef fishing, or even working a spring creek. Catching a permit on a fly is something to write home about, assuming of course that those at home have any idea of what's involved, let alone that a permit is a kind of fish and not another word for a license.

To many, this kind of fishing seems pointlessly difficult and intimidating. A friend of mine calls it my "holier than thou" kind of fishing and tells me that when

SPOTTED EAGLE RAY

Aetobatus narinari

One of the loveliest sights on the flats, these large rays "fly" slowly across your bow, the patterns of their gold and pale spots marking them in your fishing memories. They have a barbed spine on their tail, but eagle rays are not as wont as stingrays to conceal themselves.

she goes fishing she just wants to catch fish. And Woody Sexton, an old-time Keys flats guide with whom I first went tarpon fishing over twenty years ago, used to say that fly fishing for permit was really a spectator sport.

It's true we set up a bunch of rules that give the fish all kinds of advantages, but I do want to catch them. Some of my fondest memories are of sitting on the channel pier that connected White Lake with "the big lake," as we called Lake Michigan, fishing for perch just off the bottom with live minnows. Perch fishing was something I loved to do when I was ten years old, and I could recommend it to almost anyone as a pleasant way to spend a summer afternoon. It's just that now there's something else I love to do and find infinitely challenging, and, more to the point, I love the places in which I can do it. When I'm out on the flats I become that world, and I forget all about *me* and the bags I carry. It's all the life of sea and sky where "mind chains cannot clink," as Thomas Hardy has said.

But catching fish is only one small part of why I like to go fishing. The possibility of catching fish, and, in the case of permit, the improbability, are what keep my adrenaline up and my attention focused. But it's that very attention and my absorption in some of the most beautiful and abundantly fecund waters on earth that I'm seeking when I load my dog, fly rods, lunch, and, frequently, one or two of my favorite people in my sixteen-foot skiff and set off to hunt for permit, and, of course, for the slightly more cooperative though no less thrilling tarpon, bonefish, or barracuda, should they happen along.

Still, the permit's the one, precisely because it is so improbably difficult and also because, to me, it's so flat-out lovable. I'd like to adopt one and take it home as a companion for my Labrador retriever if I could figure out a way to make that work. And I'd name it Pearl after the glorious sheen of its luminous silvery skin and the beseeching expression of its conch pink lips. But since I can't do that, I think I'd like to catch one and admire it close up every once in a while.

As it turns out, the nervous water we've been watching is in fact a tailing permit, but before we can sneak within casting range, the shadow of a low-flying cormorant crosses its feeding spot and the delicate ripple becomes a purposeful bulge, much like that of a small nuclear submarine getting under way, and shoots off toward the safety of deeper water with alarming speed. I have seen fleeing permit more than a few times and continue to be awestruck by their power and acceleration. And as we watch this one, it's easy to envision how thrilling it might be to see a weight-forward white fly line ripping its impressive wake and hear the high-pitched screaming of the reel. Once again I am left with my imagination, like a fleeting glimpse of the girl of my dreams.

It had been a good morning for permit. I'd had two well-placed shots refused at the edge of a channel on the south side of this ring of islands that make up the Marquesas and two more blown with abysmal casts when I tried too hard to drive the fly into the wind and watched the leader collapse back on itself in a pathetic little heap.

Textbook casts are fairly easy for me, until the fish show up. And when you've been in the gun seat as many times as I have you ought to have learned to control the adrenaline. One morning the previous winter I had contained my excitement masterfully during three clearly observed, near perfect presentations to the same huge permit off a shore called Palm Beach on the west side of this archipelago. That fish might have run about thirty-five pounds. And when it swam decisively away after the third refusal, my right hand started shaking so violently I had to lay down my rod and eat a couple of chocolate chip cookies to keep from fainting. I also had to remind myself that what I was doing here was supposed to be fun.

And it is fun. But sometimes it feels like you're endlessly laying your heart out for the same beautiful woman, just to have it spurned. We watch the fleeing ridge of water dissolve in the rip of current where the Marquesas fall off toward Rebecca Channel, and I let out more breath than I remember having taken in.

"It's time for lunch."

Simon agrees. We stake out several hundred feet from a tiny cluster of mangroves where we can spot cruising permit while we eat our sandwiches. But since this tiny island also happens to be the principal North American rookery of the frigatebird, we end up watching the sky a good deal more than the water. There are probably three dozen "man of war" birds, as Walt Whitman called them, resting on their "prodigious pinions" a thousand feet or more above us and one which seems to be taking a particular interest in our lunch that hovers much lower. He displays his seven-and-a-half-foot wingspan, long forked tail, and brilliant orange throat pouch as if he might be trying to bargain his beauty for a bite of roast pork.

We hear terns at such a great height it seems the sky itself is calling until I locate the flock with Simon's binoculars. "There must be a hundred," I say, as I hand the glasses to Simon.

"Well, I guess that just goes to show you," Simon muses as he adjusts the focusing ring.

"Show you what?" I ask and realize instantly, I should have seen this coming.

"That one good tern deserves another."

After we pack our sandwich wrappers back in the cooler and finish off a half bag of strawberry-filled cookies, we decide to run around the north side of the Marquesas and see what we can find. On our way we speed past a basking loggerhead and glance back to see him kick over and sink into the teal green depths. We see an eagle ray make a spectacular leap and crash with great sheets of spray off our port bow and agree that, with or without fish on, this has been a spectacular day.

PERMIT

Trachinotus falcatus

Every one of the world record permit taken on a fly rod was caught off the Lower Keys, most of them in the waters off Key West. This was also the case with nearly every record permit in the all-tackle classes. Nevertheless, even in these waters, the permit is an elusive and frustrating quarry. It is also a magnificent, very strong, courageous fish.

We drop down off plane, idle up to the edge of the flat, and pole to within about fifty feet of a shore that, if it weren't protected as a national wildlife sanctuary, would be a beach developer's dream. As we parallel the white sand edge I half expect to see a rubber football or a pair of errant water wings drift by, and I'm startled to hear Simon call out: "Two fish at two o'clock. They're permit, and they're coming straight for us."

I glance over my shoulder and spot them instantly. They stand out like a couple of stainless steel baking pans in this pellucid foot-and-a-half-deep water.

"No time to set up the boat," Simon whispers. There are two good-sized fish swimming side by side a hundred feet out and closing fast. I drop my fly to the water, make two false casts toward the beach to clear the shooting head, double haul, and lay down my backcast about sixty feet behind me. It lands about six feet to the right of their approach. I'm about to pick it up and try again when Simon whispers, "Wait. They're turning on it."

I look again and can't believe what I'm seeing.

"She's going for it," Simon rasps. "She's going to eat it."

And she does too. After six years of watching permit scrutinize and decline my presentations, this particular fish in this most improbable setting is going for it like a meteor streaking for a black hole. I doubt I could have kept her away from it. I watch her close on my bogus crab, and then my leader is trailing from her mouth as she turns and bolts off toward Texas. I grasp the line with my left hand and strike her lightly to set the hook. I instinctively look down to make sure I'm not standing on the line and then realize, as she comes up tight and the reel starts screaming, that since I've done little stripping, there isn't much line to clear.

"She's on. You've got a permit on," Simon screams. Simon has taken close to a dozen permit on a fly himself, and yet he seems more excited about this one than I am.

The fish makes an initial run of about a hundred and fifty yards in the direction it came from, and its companion sticks right with it, two fleeing spirits in their argentine brilliance, streaking over the dark turtle grass. Then it turns and comes back at us, and I'm taking in line as fast as I can, trying to keep my hand rotating smoothly in the tight circumference of the reel. The other fish is gone now, having sensed something

BONNETHEAD SHARK

Sphyrna tiburo

The smallest of the flats sharks, the bonnethead averages from two to four feet in length. Easily identified by its wide, rounded head, this dark gray shark ambles across the flats and is not easily flushed by a drifting skiff. It will eat a fly, however, and once hooked has a rocketing first run.

awry when his desperate companion suddenly reversed course and headed back toward the shallows. Fifty feet from the boat, the fish turns side to, and I feel the prodigious strength of her lateral swimming. I remember how, a few years back, in conversation with a friend, we designed the perfect fighting fish and decided it would be shaped just like the scrappy, slab-sided bluegill, only bigger, much bigger. What we had come up with, we realized, was in fact, the permit.

I bend the rod low to the water to turn her to the right. Then, when she tries to swim off toward the Dry Tortugas, I work her back toward Key West. Simon positions the skiff to keep me facing her and calls to me from the poling tower, "I hope you're remembering to breathe up there."

And I do remember to breathe. I'm savoring this affair with the fish of my dreams, though, after all these rehearsals, it seems a little anticlimatic. But only a little. Pound for pound, permit are the most tenacious of fighters. I haven't gotten her to the boat yet, and I realize it could be a long time before I have another opportunity like this. She makes three more heroic runs for the open sea, a couple of last-ditch turns around the bow, and then she's lolling at the gunwhale like a tired puppy. Simon grasps the leader, then takes her gently by the tail, lifts her over the deck, and cradles her in both hands while I remove the hook from her lip.

When it's all over, when I've held her in my arms and kissed her on the forehead and Simon has taken the photograph and worked her back and forth through the water to prime her gills and released her, and we've watched her swim away, a little indifferently at first, and then, as if she's suddenly become aware of her freedom, kick in her afterburners and surge off at full speed toward the Gulf of Mexico, I feel happy and relaxed and a little sad. Something I've been seeking for a long time is over now, like a stolen weekend with a secret love. Maybe, if I'm lucky, it'll happen again. It won't be quite like the first time, but then, it never is.

STERLING SILVER

from SILENT SEASONS

Russell Chatham

HE ELEMENTAL FLATNESS OF THE FLORIDA KEYS IS COMPELLING and mysterious in its thin plane of reflective brilliance. Within their own horizontal galaxy, the flats are as inscrutable as the empyrean-blue water of the Gulf Stream itself, far outside the shoals where you look down along sharp, beveled shafts of light that narrow into blackness thousands of feet above the ocean floor.

Inshore, and out of sight of the Atlantic's barrier reefs, among the very Keys themselves, the horizon is often lost somewhere behind refulgent bands of light and shimmering heat waves. On certain hot, humid days without wind, distant mangrove islands are seen only as extraneous tubes of gray-green, lying inexplicably in the silver atmosphere like alien spaceships.

Over in the backcountry, the Gulf side of the Keys, long plateaus of uneven coral stall the tide and agitate it so the waterscape vibrates and sparkles. The whole of this inside territory is an unfathomably complex tapestry of radical design.

Few people understand that this vast district is one of the great wildernesses of North America. Travelers, as they fly between Marathon Key or Key West and Miami, are temporarily enthralled by the complicated pattern of lime-green channels and basins, the ochre and light-sienna coral and sand flats, the islands. But almost no one ever *goes there*.

Most of those who do have occupational reasons: sponge, lobster and conch fishermen, shrimpers, and fishing guides. Groups of bird watchers sometimes visit certain

special keys. Skin divers occasionally get out and poke around old wrecks. And lastly, there are sportsmen.

Even within this last category is bracketed yet another minority within the minority: a fisherman who, in the opinion of some, carries it too far, bringing with him restyled nineteenth-century attitudes, seemingly inappropriate equipment and a full-on desire to proceed without secondary motives. Sometimes alone, sometimes with a close friend or perhaps a sympathetic hired guide, with benefit of only a small open skiff, a pole to push it, a fly rod and a perverse desire to be out of fashion, he goes out there to fish for tarpon.

It takes leisure time and a nature disposed toward contemplation, and sometimes contradiction, to develop passion for pastimes with surface pointlessness. In the instance of fly fishing for tarpon, a certain quantum of cash on hand is also required, although in no way is this an endeavor suited to the idle rich, or for that matter, to anyone else slightly dotty. You need all your faculties.

Suppose you have the time, the money and the faculties. Assuming you want to expend them all on exotic fishing, why would you choose to go for tarpon rather than, say, marlin, a historically much more glamorous quarry? Enter your aforementioned contemplative, sometimes contradictory character.

If you think about distilling *fishing* down to *angling,* then further, to angling's diamond center, you can scarcely come to any conclusion other than this: as the time immediately preceding that point at which the fish actually becomes hooked grows more difficult, intense and all-absorbing, the quality of the fishing improves.

After that, you want the take to be hard to manage—fascinating in and of itself—and the ensuing struggle to be, above all, noble. Now, these moments may follow so closely upon one another they seem as one, yet there remains a hierarchy, however blurred. Then, way down there at the bottom of the list, is the dead fish on your hands.

"SLICK CALM MORNING" *Peter Corbin*

To catch a marlin you must troll. Say the word over and over again to yourself, drawing it out as if it were spelled with lots of o's and l's. There may be nothing on earth, except perhaps an unsuccessful bridge-club luncheon, quite so boring as trolling. Trol-l-l-l-ing. Several hours of it should be enough to dull your senses so that when the captain or mate or speed of the boat, or whatever it is, finally hooks a fish and you are faced with the appalling prospect of an hour in the fighting chair, you simply would rather have a beer.

On quite another hand, nowhere else in the spectrum of available angling can there be found a more profoundly thrilling prelude to the hooking of a fish than in the stalking of tarpon in shallow water. The fly rod ups the ante considerably, too. In short, it's at least twice as much trouble as any other tackle you could use.

On the flats, where you must *see* everything, the search becomes an alarmingly patent and suspenseful intrigue. This game calls for a blend of refined skills, those of the hunter as well as the fisherman. It is a process, an experience, to which few, if any, ever really become fully initiated.

This is one of those spring mornings you always hope for: still, humid and already warm, so that the guides at the Sea Center of Big Pine Key feel the air and call it a tarpon day. As you ease out of the cut, enormous clouds are stacked around the horizon, nacreous and pillowy. Later a breeze may rise out of the southwest, but now the water is slick as mercury, its pastel patina reflecting the tops of the tallest clouds.

You are two days into a series of spring tides. This means you will be able to fish places that have been neglected during the preceding weeks, when there was not enough of a flood to bring the tarpon in. The plan will be to stake certain corners, then later, pole out some other banks.

When you shut down at your first stop it is suddenly as still as a room. The pole is taken from its chocks and your companion begins moving you into a higher

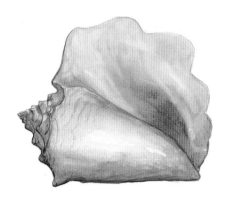

QUEEN CONCH

Strombus gigas

The resource that gave Lower Keys natives their nickname, the conch is now a fully protected species. Hunted both for its meat and the rich, pink hues of its large shell, the conch all but vanished from the flats. Now, however, if you're lucky, you can see them here and there as you drift in your skiff. Look, but do not touch.

position. It is still early, the sun at too oblique an angle to give real visibility yet.

Already it is getting hot, the high humidity causing a haze to form. It is impossible to see anything of the bottom beyond a few yards and you wonder how your friend knows where to stake. He is looking for the *corner*, he says, but you can notice no variation whatsoever in the even carpet of turtle grass.

Shortly, he pushes the stake in and ties off. You get up on the casting deck. Fish will be coming up the bank on your right, then cutting across where you are staked.

You pull off enough line for a throw, make one, then coil the running line neatly at your feet. You hold the fly in your hand, leaving a loop of fly line in the water long enough for a false cast. Now you wait and look.

There is plenty of time to think about the shortcomings of your fly casting, the different ways you might blow the chance when it comes. Your feet start to ache and you shift them a little so that later when you look down to make sure the fly line is not tangled, you see you're standing on it. You cast and recoil it carefully.

"Rollers. Hundred yards."

You look with extra intensity at the indefinite sheen as if the harder you stare the more likely you are to see something. Then they glint in unison, closer, and are gone again. The first wave of fright settles into your abdomen.

They're coming just as we thought. This way. Up the bank. Where are they? Where are they! It's not too soon to false cast. Get going. Oh no. No! They're right here. At the boat. Flushing.

The frightened fish are scooting away, back into the sheen. There are marl muds everywhere around the boat, and the boils the fish make as they depart seem to send a shiver beneath the skiff you can feel on the bottoms of your feet. You wish you had your blanket and a bottle of Jergens lotion.

Several other pods of tarpon work their way up the tide. Always, though, their trajectory takes them past the skiff out of range. In an hour the surge of fish seems to have passed, gone on to Loggerhead or wherever they were going. You decide to pull the stake and pole out to the bank.

As your companion begins to pole, you wish the sun would climb higher, the haze dissipate. You offer to take the pole, are turned down.

The drab grasses tilt in the slow current like a billion signposts gone wrong. Poling, you will be obliged to concern yourself with trigonometry: moving tide, moving boat, moving fish, degree of intercept.

Without notice, basins appear, deep and crisply emerald over their white sand bottoms. Sometimes there are barracuda arranged in them like dark lines of doom.

Small, tan sharks glide past the boat; rays, too, moving over the flat as the tide floods. The bank is 1,000 yards long. Somewhere on its easy slope there must be tarpon. You surge smoothly forward, transom first, that gentle sound being the only one you hear. Three hundred, 400 yards. Nothing.

What a strange way to fish this is. You might be out here for eight hours, running the boat ten, maybe twenty miles, and you never lose sight of the bottom. A drastic change in depth, one that might mean fish instead of no fish, or an easy pass through a little green cut rather than a grounded skiff or sheared pin, is twelve inches. Coming down off a plane at thirty knots at the wrong moment can mean settling into the grass so you will have to get out and push the heavy skiff until the bottom slopes away enough to get back in and pole your way out of it.

Down here they always tell you, if something goes wrong with the engine, just get out and walk home.

"Twelve o'clock. Way out." Quite far ahead, you see the chain of sparkles as tarpon roll, gulping air.

NURSE SHARK

Ginglymostoma cirratum

This is the shark species you are most likely to see as you move across the flats. Most often it appears asleep on the bottom, a sluggish, reddish-brown shark with a broad snout and barbels under its chin. Relatively nonaggressive, the nurse shark won't take lures and is generally a lazy predator.

Tarpon on the bank. Hundred and fifty yards? Hundred? Can't let them get too close. Stay in front of the first fish. Are there two? Six? A dozen? Nothing. Sheen. Reflection. Haze. Useless glasses.

Boat's closing. Fish coming on. Remember. Fly in hand. Ready. Loop of line trailing. Glance to see it's not back in the way of the pole. Fly line still coiled. Loose. Strain your eyes. Look. Wakes? They're colder gray. Light. And dark. Not warm, not tan like the bottom. Movement will tell. Long. They're long, cool gray. Temples pound. The glare, relentless. Sheen. No shapes. No gray. Another wake. Still farther out than you thought. Never mind. Roll the line. Think about it. Streamer gone, in the air. Back loop flat . . . not so tight! Slow down. There he is, within range, rolling, enormous scales catching the light. Your friend is urging, warning. Now! Wait out the backcast. Don't dump it. Wait. Drift. Know the intercept. Correct. Don't change direction too much. Not too much drive. Ease the cast off. Strip hard. Get his eye. Strip. A wake. Water rushing, churning. A take! Stay balanced, feel the turn, the tension. Now strike! Again, to the side. Again. Don't look up. Watch the line clear itself. Tarpon's in the air. Eye level, upside down, twisting, rattling. Push slack. Running. Too fast. Another jump. Gone.

Tarpon are not used as food. You would think there must be some way they might be thus prepared, but they just aren't eaten. Nor are they taken for other commercial reasons. At one time there was a scheme to convert them to pet food or fertilizer, a plan fortunately abandoned. In any case, there is no price per pound for tarpon, and no diners sit fidgeting with their utensils while their tarpon fillets are being broiled.

On the other side of the ledger, this has come to mean a lack of sound information about the fish and its habits. Tarpon are thought to be migratory, moving from south to north and from salt to brackish or fresh water as part of their spawning cycle. They also travel from deep to shallow water, ostensibly to feed. However, a true species pattern is not clearly known.

To the fish's broadest advantage, this also means there is no wholly justifiable cause for anyone to kill one. Those slight reasons used center entirely around man's own vanity. Fishermen may cart them to the dock, but the only one truly bringing them home is the Southernmost Scavenger Service. The flimsy excuses, then, for killing tarpon rest in that zone somewhere between the charterman's only ad a tourist will buy and the Kodak dealer.

It's possible to intrude upon the larger spirit of fishing in any number of ways besides pointlessly killing the animal. Not the least of these is to destroy the privacy. For example, hardly anything can ruin the tranquility of a day's fishing like a good tournament. The reason keeps turning out to be greed in one form or another, with slices of unresolved ego gratification thrown in for good measure.

It's becoming practically un-American to disapprove of fishing tournaments these days. But if you take an affable, essentially noncompetitive, harmless activity, the principal attribute of which lies in the quality of the time spent pursuing it rather than in the grossness of the last results, and you begin giving large cash prizes for the grossest last results, suddenly it's all gone.

Some negate the magic of angling by approaching it from a standpoint of overt, even bizarre practicality: equipment specifications, a humorless concern over questions that have only numbers as answers.

What hook size to use? What percentage of the point should be triangulated? What pound test should the weakest leader section be? What pound-class world record do you want to qualify for? How long should the whole leader be? The butt section? What size line? What's its diameter in thousandths of an inch? How long are its tapers? The belly? How thin is the running line? How much of it is there? How long is the rod? How heavy? How many yards of backing on the reel? What pound test? How tight do you set the reel drag? How long is the boat? How much does it weigh? Its beam? How much water does it draw? How fast does it go? What horsepower is the engine? What's the capacity of the gas tank? How long is the push pole? How many knots can you tie? How far can you cast? How high is the tide? What time do you start fishing? What year is it? How many points do you get for a keeper in the Islamorada Invitational Fly Championship? How much do Minimum Qualifiers count per pound? How much do releases count? If you caught a 73-pounder, a 104-pounder, three releases and a 90-pounder with cheese, what would you have? A large hamburger?

Everyone addresses a certain number of technical questions, but it seems this can be done cursorily, and as a matter of light concern. Attention to facts and figures as if they were really important often obscures the things of real importance, things that cannot be counted, recorded or even clearly explained. In final analysis, those things will appear as states of mind, wordless, indescribable and of a dimension altogether intangible.

If you are going to replace the essential quietude of fishing with semi-industrial or businesslike considerations, it might be more sensible, simpler and certainly cheaper never to leave the office.

It is now early afternoon and you are being poled downlight over a brilliant, white-sand bottom. Much of the earlier haze has cleared and visibility is now extraordinary. Actually, you're just offshore from a low, tropical-looking key which shimmers in the heat, its long beaches curving nearly out of view.

Swells from the Atlantic roll the skiff so that it is important to remain keenly balanced. You are in about eight feet of water, somewhat on the deep side for fly casting to cruising fish, particularly if they are near the bottom. As you shift your weight with the motion of the boat, the Cuban-mix sandwich and three Gatorades you so hastily challenged for lunch press heavily against your tee shirt.

You are in the middle of a long corridor of stark, bright bottom. On your right is the island; on your left, perhaps 100 yards away, the sand abruptly ending against low coral; there is a thin irregular line of green, breakers and then blue water. Once, you see an enormous hammerhead cruising the edge.

Visibility is so perfect there is no need to be on the alert for the surprise appearance of tarpon anywhere within a 200-foot radius of the skiff. If it came within fly casting distance, a three-pound barracuda would look like a Greyhound Scenicruiser.

It is troublesome poling in the deep water, not only because of that very fact, but because the bottom is quite hard, so the pole makes a clunking sound when it's put down. The foot of the pole doesn't grab well either, slipping off ineffectually behind the boat.

You and your companion see the dark spots at the same time. There is a moment of hesitation, then it suddenly becomes clear they are tarpon even though they are still very far off. You will have a full three minutes to try and get the upper hand on your mounting nervousness.

Were we wrong? No, they're tarpon all right. Eight, maybe ten. All big—seventy, eighty pounds and better. Still very far. Funny how the school changes shape. They string out, bunch up. Fish must be very foreshortened at this distance. So clear. Almost like watching birds flying. Watch footing. Is the fly line tangled? School's turning. Traveling closer to the key. Boat's turning. Good. Must intercept them. Must take them head on. Too deep for a side shot. They'd see the boat. It's going to work. Looking at them from in front.

"I'm down. Anytime." You look back and your friend has the push pole flat across his knees. "Go." He insists, never taking his eyes from the tarpon.

How far now? Hundred-fifty feet. False casting. Hold up all the line you can. Fish coming on, almost single-file. Watch. You want thirty feet on them. No slips. Loops open. Controlled. Cast. Wait. Fly settling. Two, three feet. Tarpon at six. Or eight. Closing. Is the lead fish close enough? Start bringing it back. He sees it. Accelerating. Elevating. Growing silver. Face disjointing. Dark. Has it. Turning back down. Tension. Hit hard. Again. Again. Again.

He is already going another way and the strain disorients you so much the fly line is suddenly gone from your left hand. Whirling, it jams its way through the guides. You hear the sound of the power tilt as the engine goes down, starts. Slowly, you begin to follow.

TARPON FISHING: THE FIRST THIRTY SECONDS

Jeffrey Cardenas

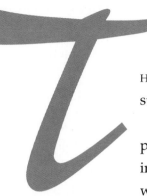

HIS IS THE MOMENT IN SALTWATER FLY FISHING WHEN ALL TIME stands still.

You have studied the school of tarpon as your guide positioned the skiff for your shot. The fish are astonishingly beautiful gliding toward you through the clear water. Rolling slowly to the surface, the early morning light reflects off their backs like a series of camera flashes. As the fish get closer, a tarpon's giant eye—Megalops—meets yours and it is unnerving. Lucid and clear. *What does it see?*

Maybe you have watched the fish too long . . . your mouth is dry; your knees no longer seem to support the weight of your body. There is a nervous twitch in your casting arm. You have been waiting a long time for this opportunity. You've probably spent several thousand dollars to bring you to this moment. You've watched all the videos and read all the books. You're geared up, psyched up. You are ready.

At least you *think* you are.

The next thirty seconds will be either the most exciting or the most exasperating half minute of your life.

The cast has to be on target. The strip must fool the fish; this is *angling,* it's not automatic. When the tarpon elevates, accelerates, and takes the fly, what follows is like a dream sequence you will relive many times—whether you want to or not. So many things happen at once and none of them is predictable. The moment the

JEFFREY CARDENAS

tarpon feels steel all bets are off. You must be prepared to think on several levels simultaneously. The hook must be decisively set. The line must be cleared. You must have the presence of mind to bow on those initial jumps or the game is over before it has begun.

Once the fly line is on the reel it's time to start breathing again. Your rod is bent double and the reel drag is singing as the fish heads for Cuba, but you have won a minor victory. You have survived the first thirty seconds of fly fishing for tarpon, and the guide didn't have to call your cardiologist on the VHF radio.

The cast to a tarpon takes on so many different forms that it is essential for an angler to be fluent in a range of presentations. The fish can appear suddenly out of the glare and you'll have only a couple of seconds to make your cast. More often you will see tarpon coming from a distance and you can use that time to make a cohesive plan of attack—or you can crumble under the pressure like a piece of stale bread.

An angler I know (who now fishes alone) once told me of a companion who would take his turn on the bow with the outward appearance of having everything under control. The fly line was stripped out into neat coils on the deck. A proper length of line extended beyond his rod tip to make that first cast quick and easy. The fly was held lightly on the bend of the hook between his thumb and forefinger. This angler was ready—he was cool, cocky, and confident. Even his hair was perfect. And then the fish came into view. The first sign of impending disaster was that his Adam's apple would start to pulsate in his throat. You could see it bobbing up and down like a yo-yo in his neck. He'd adjust his hat and sunglasses. Then he would adjust them again. Almost unconsciously, he would start to rock his rod tip back and forth, enough so that the line extending from the tip would flip over in a single wrap. In a hurry, he would whip the rod around to unwrap the line and he'd put a couple fresh wraps going the opposite direction. Then he'd become confused about which way the line was fouled. Now, in a panic, he'd shake his rod like a wet dog and the line would braid into a hopeless snarl of twists and knots. This poor fellow would be clawing at the mess while the school of tarpon streamed past within an arm's length on both sides of the skiff.

Rule number one: Relax. Don't hyperventilate. This is just fishing. Take it easy and you'll find that you can cast as well to a tarpon on the flats as you do when you are practice casting to targets in your backyard. Cast beyond and in front of the fish so that you strip an intercept that will bring the fly to within inches of the tarpon's nose. Remember that getting the fly to the tarpon's depth is essential. Sure, the fish will rise to take a fly, but they'd much rather have their food delivered on a silver platter. Tarpon are opportunistic eaters. West of Key West, the tarpon feed primarily on shrimp. A hundred-twenty-pound tarpon needs to eat a lot of shrimp to satisfy a huge appetite, but it usually won't expend much energy to chase one down.

Rule number two: Don't make the tarpon have to work to take the fly. Deliver it to the table.

Watching a tarpon eat is one of the great joys of nature. A tarpon will first show that it has taken notice of a fly with a quivering of the pectoral fins. The fish's entire attitude changes. Its body becomes rigid. It moves out of cadence with other fish in the school. The tarpon is *lighting up.* Many times this happens quite slowly. The tarpon's tail swings a few extra beats as it tracks the fly. Those big eyes lock onto its prey. The take usually comes with a slight acceleration. The gills flare and a powerful vacuum causes the fly literally to vanish into the tarpon's mouth. One moment the fly is there and the tarpon is a foot away from it; the next moment the fly is gone and the fish is turned.

If you are lucky enough to see the tarpon's mouth open you will notice that its lower mandible extends far beyond the upper gape of its jaw. This is a superior mouth. The fit of its jaws is perfect when they are closed and water resistance on the fish is minimal. With its mouth open, however, the tarpon's head has the hydrodynamics of a bucket. The fish no longer has a smooth tracking ability, but the bucket mouth is drawing in a huge volume of water and not much escapes if the tarpon wants to eat it.

From the perspective on the bow of the boat you should be prepared for things to get lively.

The set is really the moment of truth. When you have had the opportunity to watch a tarpon eat your fly, it takes incredible self-restraint not to strike too soon. You wait for your moment. The tarpon's mouth *must* be closed or your fly will reappear as quickly as it vanished. Your fly is swirling around in several gallons of water inside the tarpon's mouth. You must continue stripping to find the inside of the tarpon's mouth. The hook will not find something to stick into unless *you make it happen*. Once your fly meets resistance it is time to get down to business.

If you have stripped the line tight there is no slack to rob your strike. Your stripping hand and rod should pull back in different directions. You may get in one good lick, but if the fish continues toward you it is imperative that you strip tight again before giving the tarpon another jab. Don't try to nail the hook home on your first strike. Let the fly get set up in the tarpon's mouth and then strike repeatedly. It's like hammering a nail into a piece of wood. The hammering starts lightly and then finishes progressively stronger.

Of course, if somebody was hammering a nail into my mouth I wouldn't be sitting still for it. Anticipate unpredictability. The next several moments are why you are here.

The run is never the same twice. For any description of a tarpon's behavior there is an equally valid contradiction. Most of the time when a tarpon feels the hook it goes

"TARPON'S TEMPEST" *Peter Corbin*

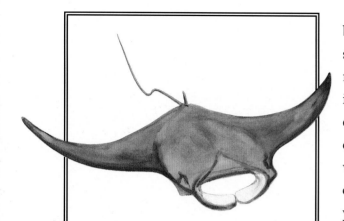

MANTA RAY

Manta birostris

These docile creatures have been misnamed devil fish and devil rays. They can reach twenty-two feet from wingtip to wingtip, but those most likely to be seen in the channels between flats are smaller and a lovely sight when they leap clear of the surface and fall back with a wild splash of white water.

berserk. The fish is probably thinking about its perennial nemesis the hammerhead shark when, from its perspective, things begin to go wrong. The initial acceleration is mind-bending. Tarpon have incredible power in their tail, and you feel every ounce of it on the first run. The fly line that was placed so neatly at your feet now takes on a life of its own. Clearing the line on a hot tarpon is a panic—I don't care how many you've caught. Your control (or lack of it) comes from the amount of tension you give the fish with your clearing hand. If your grip on the line is too loose, you are relinquishing all control over the situation and you might as well sit down before you hurt yourself. If your grip is too tight, you'll pop off the fish (if you're lucky) or the line will cut through your fingers like a band-saw blade. If you apply uneven clearing pressure, the fly line is going to spring off the deck like a witch, and you'll have the knot from hell mashed up in your first stripping guide.

We all know the disasters that can befall us if the line coming off the deck is wrapped around your tackle bag, your rod butt, or your body. The line is going out so fast that is seems there is little time to think; sometimes you can only react.

The most memorable line-clearing disaster happened once when I had two of the best trout fishermen in the world tarpon fishing with me in the Marquesas. One angler was experienced with tarpon. The other guy was still waiting for his first big fish. When the shot finally came the experienced angler coached his buddy through every step of the presentation. After the take he cleared his line cleanly until, at the very end, the angler realized he had stepped through a loop. Meanwhile, his experienced friend picked up the video camera to document the fun. The line came tight in a figure-eight knot around the angler's foot and took him down to the deck like a professional wrestler. Sixteen-pound tippet doesn't break all that easily. I remember the angler yelling to this buddy, "Help me get if off my foot! Take off my shoe!" The video, however, was too good for the expert to pass up, and he kept filming while the line tightened like a wire rabbit snare around his buddy's ankle. Finally the tippet popped. "That's tarpon fishing!" said the expert, putting down his video camera. "Now reel up, it's my shot."

The jump of a tarpon on a fly is one of the great moments in sport. There is nothing else in angling even remotely like the sight of a big tarpon clearing the water at close range. Above all else you notice the tarpon's head. It breaks the surface of the water with startling fury. Most of what you see is a blur because the shaking is so violent. The armored gill plates flare and the gill rakers rattle like amplified castanets. When the fish clears the water the body doesn't usually follow the direction of the head. The two parts appear to move independently. The aerial contortions seem unbelievable and yet they are happening right in front of your face.

A. J. McClane once said, "In shallow water a tarpon has nowhere to go but straight up." The first series of jumps is so erratic that the angler's response must be purely reflexive. I've seen a tarpon take close at nine o'clock on the port side of the skiff and then jump seconds later at three o'clock on the starboard side. In this case the fly rod was dragged into the gunwale and it exploded like a pipe bomb. Another time a tarpon took an angler's fly fifteen feet off the bow of the skiff and made its first jump *over* the poling platform on the stern, knocking me off like a bowling pin. The next jump landed on the back deck, and the angler suddenly found himself sharing the skiff with a frenzied tarpon while his guide was treading water and nursing a thump to the head.

Under normal circumstances (although tarpon fishing is hardly ever normal) the line elevates in anticipation of a jump. Frequently this occurs while you are setting the hook and clearing the line. If the jump catches you unaware, you will probably lose the fish. You have to give yourself room to bow when the fish comes up. This can be difficult to remember in the heat of the moment because during the strip and the take your rod tip is low to the water and pointed directly at the fish. If the fish jumps when your rod is at this angle you have nothing to give. Lift your rod tip in anticipation of the jump. Bring your elbows close to your body so that they can spring forward when the fish comes up. Technically, the move should be described as a reach instead of a bow. You don't want to throw ten feet of slack into the jump; you just want to relieve some of the line tension so the tarpon's head thrashing won't pull the hook. After the fish has landed, remember to recoil your elbows close to your body and raise the rod tip. You want to be prepared for a double jump. If you are standing with your mouth open and your arms extended, congratulating yourself for remembering to bow on the first jump, the tarpon will inevitably re-jump and you'll be left holding a limp fly line.

Those first thirty seconds are why we fly fish for tarpon. That initial rush of adrenaline is intoxicating. It is intellectually stimulating to think on so many levels simultaneously. In this careful and predictable world there is an attraction to having something in nature bring you to the edge of being out of control. There is no room here for error, and that's what makes it so much fun.

After the first series of jumps the battle becomes a tug-of-war. There *is* skill necessary in determining the leverage and pull that will bring the fish to the side of the skiff. Occasionally you get a late jump, so you have to stay on your toes. But the release of the tarpon can be anticlimactic. The fish is whipped. You chalk one up on the scoreboard, but somehow this is the part of tarpon fishing that seems to carry less importance. When you sit back in the afterglow and consider what just happened, the dogged fight and the capture of this great fish are not what you will immediately recall. What you *will* remember, and what you'll tell your children about, are those first thirty seconds when time stood still.

BLANTON'S BEACH PARTY

from WHERE IS JOE MERCHANT?

Jimmy Buffett

HE WIND WHISTLED THROUGH THE WINDING STAIRCASE OF Sand Key Lighthouse, making the girders and support cables groan and twang like a gigantic wind chime. Blanton was in the room that housed the batteries for the signal lamp up above. It was familiar territory. He thought of the lighthouse and the tiny spit of land around it as his backyard. As a kid, he had fished and snorkeled nearby, in a place where the greens of the shallow water gave way to the deep blue patterns of the Gulf Stream. In his teenage years, he had learned the secrets of a woman's body on this small island that came and went with the currents of the stream.

Debris of all kinds was scattered across the floor, and a collage of graffiti covered the walls. Blanton walked to the metal hatch on the opposite side of the room and pulled it open.

Outside, big rollers, unfamiliar to these waters, washed across the hazardous coral canyons of the reef, and Blanton looked down at his old flats skiff. After escaping the scene of the explosion, he had sped directly north until he knew he was out of sight of any witness. He had circled west to the Marquesas Keys and then south to Sand Key. He had always been amazed at how well his little skiff functioned in rough weather. The boat was now hidden below, tied to the catwalk with several spring lines.

Blanton had towed one of the Jet Skis with him. It bobbed up and down erratically in the sea like a spoiled brat, and Blanton wondered why fate had cursed him and had hung this high-tech albatross around his neck. Yesterday he had been just another crazy flats guide, but this morning he was a wanted man.

MAGNIFICENT FRIGATEBIRD

Fregata magnificens

Perched in trees in the Marquesas, frigatebirds are black ovals strung like obsidian beads along the branches. But overhead, in the air, with their great wings spread and their forked tails wide, frigatebirds become the consummate fliers of the Keys.

When Jet Skis first showed up in the keys, all the guides bitched about them. They served no useful purpose and made a hideous noise that sent the fish in a five-mile radius scurrying off the flats into deep water for shelter. They disrupted the nesting of the shore birds in the mangroves, and they were dangerous torpedoes in the hands of the incompetent people who rented them.

Blanton's frustration with the Jet Skis had turned violent one day. He was fishing an older client on the flats just north of Boca Grande, and they were hooked up to a giant tarpon. For nearly two hours, Blanton had coached the inexperienced angler through the fatigue of fighting such a big fish, and finally the client had turned the fish's head toward the boat. This meant the tarpon was tired. About twenty feet from the boat, the big tarpon made a desperate run, which carried him about a hundred feet from the boat. The fisherman was exhausted and fell to the floor of the skiff.

Blanton muscled the big fish alongside the boat, grabbed him by the tail, and moved him back and forth to force water through his gills. He felt the tail come alive, and when he released his grip, the fish swam slowly away on the surface. In a few seconds, he would catch his breath and dive for the shelter of the deep water.

From out of nowhere, two hotshots on Jet Skis came roaring across the flats and circled Blanton's skiff. The big tarpon never knew what hit him. The Jet Skis sped off in the direction of the island, and Blanton poled his skiff to the fish, which was now floating on the surface. Its head had been crushed, and the blood had already attracted a school of small bonnet sharks.

In twenty years of guiding, Blanton had never killed a tarpon. Every fish that found its way onto a line from his boat was revived after the encounter and sent back to the ocean. Now Blanton pulled the big fish into the boat and headed for Boca Grande, following the scattered wakes of the two Jet Skis.

He circled past the point where the Jet Skiers were having a party, then idled over to a little stretch of beach he called his "thinking spot." He gave the fisherman a candy bar and a Coke and told him to rest nearby in the shade of a palmetto. Then Blanton dug a hole in the sand and buried the tarpon. He combed the beach for driftwood and debris and erected a makeshift monument. Using an old piece of charcoal from a long-extinguished campfire, he wrote an inscription on the plank:

Here lies a great fish killed by a Jet Ski.

Blanton took the fisherman back to town and then returned to the island, where the beach party was in full swing. He sneaked through the mangroves, grabbed the ghetto blaster, and drop-kicked it into the water. Then he began to beat the living shit out of the two guys who had killed the tarpon. He set their Jet Skis on fire and went back to town and turned himself in to the sheriff.

Blanton was arrested, and charges were pressed. He was sentenced to six months and was made to pay for the Jet Skis he had burned. He served his time and had just been released from jail the week before.

"I'm not sayin' it's okay to do what I did—things just got out of hand. But I guess what I'm trying to say is that I feel about the flats the way the Sioux Indians feel about the Black Hills. They're sacred, and when I see them abused, I react. I'm a territorial son of a bitch. I consider Tell Tale Cut *my* flat."

YOUTHFUL REALITIES

George Reiger

'M A SURVIVOR OF A FORGOTTEN TIME. I'M ONE OF A DWINDLING NUMBER of people who remember when Marathon was little more than a bus stop and a bait shop, and when respectable people regarded Key West as an unsavory haunt of human flotsam and jetsam despite or, perhaps, because of Harry Truman's occasional visits. (Come to think of it, respectable people still think that.)

Tourists were rare in the lower Keys in the late 1940s. A few college kids showed up mostly to say they'd driven as far south as it was possible to go. They poked around town—sometimes only standing in the entrance of a bar to peer inside—then got in their cars for the long haul back to Miami.

In those days, the Keys were inhabited primarily by wreckers, renegades, and wealthy sportsmen. Key Largo's Ocean Reef Club—where my father took his three sons—was only the latest variation on angling fraternities dating back to the turn of the century. Like the Long Key Fishing Camp—established in 1906 and extinguished by the hurricane of 1935—the Ocean Reef Club, founded more than a decade later, was located near prime bonefish flats. Also like the Long Key Fishing Camp, most members of the Ocean Reef Club came to fish the Gulf Stream, not the flats.

When my father met Ernest Hemingway, they talked about billfish, not bonefish. Years later, when I visited the tourist trap that Hemingway's Key West home had become, I was amused to see on a bookcase below a small mounted tarpon, a saltwater fly reel. Hemingway might have caught such a tarpon for shark bait, but he would not have done so on a fly reel. Anglers of his generation used fly tackle in fresh water and drums filled with 24- and 36-thread line in salt.

41

When an angler today pictures himself fishing the Keys, he imagines a heroic figure with a fly rod (or a less heroic figure with spinning tackle) poised in the bow of a streamlined fishing machine, while his equally heroic guide strains with a push pole to intercept a pod of tailing (fill in the blank) a) tarpon b) bonefish c) permit.

But that's not my image, nor my youthful reality. For one thing, most people I remember who fished the flats in the 1940s were there only because it was blowing too hard to be offshore. I'm amused today when I hear anglers say their flats vacation was ruined by wind. As kids, the main reason we spent time on the flats at all was to salvage what we could from windy days. Poling or rowing a plywood skiff through roiled, ruffled, and occasionally white-capped water was preferable to taking green seas over the bow of a charter boat in the Gulf Stream. Had my father been on his own, he would probably have spent those days reading mysteries in his room at the Ocean Reef Club. But with three boys to look after, the flats represented a kind of panoramic playground.

My brothers and I loved messing around on the flats, partly because it was a world Dad didn't much care about and which we could stake out as our own, and partly because most everything from water depth to fish size was on a scale more in keeping with our youthful expectations.

Writing in 1922, Zane Grey mused about "the mystery of bonefishing." After stating "I have never been able to tell why it seems the fullest, the most difficult, the strangest and most thrilling, the lonesomest and most all-satisfying of all kinds of angling," Grey decided it's because "in bonefishing there is more of a return to boyish emotions" than in any other kind of fishing.

Since my brothers and I were boys, we didn't yearn to "return to boyish emotions." We, also, didn't think as highly of bonefish as Zane Grey did since we'd been indoctrinated with the idea that their highest and best use was as marlin bait. Indeed,

BALLYHOO

Hemiramphus brasiliensis

Like the glass minnow, known as mahua in the Keys, the ballyhoo was apparently designed to be eaten by almost every other fish. Slim and silver touched with brilliant blue, these shimmering cigars are never still. Sometimes their schools explode in panic, a shining rain that falls upwards.

my older brother and I had caught countless dozens of bonefish for precisely that purpose.

Tony and I had also caught dozens of tarpon—mostly by trolling spoons in the St. Lucie River near Stuart—so we didn't get particularly excited when we saw a chain of Silver King wending its way across a flat. Besides, it was popularly believed at the time that shallow-water tarpon were too spooky to catch. If you wanted tarpon, you used live bait in the channels or under the highway bridges at night.

Of today's Big Three of the Flats, we held the permit in the highest esteem because they were an uncommon prize, fought like the dickens, and were delicious to eat. We released most every tarpon and bonefish we caught (except bonefish we planned to use for bait), but we kept every permit. Averaging better than twenty pounds each, permit were for us a kind of super-sized pompano with all the gustatory connotations of that species.

Overall, we were more interested in big fish and curiosities than game fish. We thrilled to the imagined dangers of hunting sharks and stingrays with a gig. We loved wading and diving for the still abundant conch and spiny lobster. We got so tired of eating lobster, we once took our catch out on the reef at night, twisted off the lobsters' heads and smashed them up for chum with an old Louisville Slugger. Then we used the tails to catch the largest yellowtail snappers I've ever seen.

Our greatest prizes were jewfish found in blue holes and under bridges. They were so powerful it was hard to hold them on rod and reel. We preferred a handline of war-surplus parachute cord, a cable leader, and a car-tire inner-tube to absorb the fish's sudden lunges. I've seen jewfish stretch such snubbers twelve feet.

An anchored rowboat was a poor jewfishing platform because a big fish would simply drag it around until the anchor caught on a coral ledge—whereupon the fish would promptly pull the skiff underwater, unless someone was quick enough to cut the line. My older brother became obsessed with jewfishing and made quite a science of it. He preferred fishing from bridges and found that saltwater catfishes were his hardiest live baits. He first clipped the catfish's spiny dorsal and pectoral fins and ran a wire through its back where most fishermen would have inserted the hook. He then haywire-twisted the curve of the hook to the catfish's back so it rode parallel with the backbone, point forward. Rigged like that, his baits—even large mullet—would stay alive, swimming in the current, all night long.

I don't recall a jewfish Tony caught in the Keys that was much over 200 pounds, but we later used his technique on the St. Lucie River to land some notable brutes, including a 440-pounder. The drawbacks to Keys' jewfishing were that hooked fish were sometimes attacked by huge sharks, and that perfectly good jewfish baits were occasionally mauled by pesky tarpon.

Another youthful pastime was dapping for needlefish. Small houndfish (alias, needlefish) could be found in the lee of practically every piling or mangrove island in the Keys. On windy days, we'd let the breeze catch our line—at the end of which we had a tiny plug of shrimp with an even tinier hook inside—and skate or skip the bait over the surface near a houndfish waiting at the edge of an eddy. The houndfish would chase down and seize the bait with its toothy beak. We gave the fish slack until it had swum around and swallowed the hook. When we struck, the houndfish tail-walked and somersaulted with all the gusto of a miniature marlin.

Since we really had no use for houndfish—unlike bonefish and ballyhoo, they make a poor trolling bait—and although we later learned that big ones are filletable and quite good to eat despite the greenish gray color of their raw flesh—we eventually did our dapping without any hooks at all. We'd play keep away to tease the houndfish into such a frenzy that when they finally caught the bait, they'd wolf it down and were sometimes caught, even without a hook.

Of all the Keys' denizens that delighted us (but were spurned by more ambitious anglers), none was more dependable than the barracuda. No matter how umpromising the day, we could always find a barracuda to spice our outing with adventure. Purists who came to fish the flats for "quality" species were slow to appreciate the barracuda's worth, but businessmen across the country had already begun to realize the fish's toothy appeal. In addition to mounting barracuda for anglers who'd caught them, taxidermist Al Pflueger found a growing market among executives who'd buy barracuda for their office walls to inspire admiration and awe among clients and competition. Pflueger paid Ocean Reef Club guide Tommy Gifford for all the barracuda he sent by ice truck to Miami, and Tommy tapped the Reiger boys to help him catch them. To show his appreciation for our assistance, Pflueger mounted a trophy-size rainbow runner (an uncommon catch in the Atlantic) that my younger brother, John, had landed, which hung over the bar of the Ocean Reef Club for many years.

In 1970, I was the boating and outdoors editor for *Popular Mechanics* and had met the chief executive officer of a company that made aluminum houseboats. The CEO

FLYING FISH

Cypsilurus heterurus

This Atlantic flying fish is more at home in deeper ocean waters just off the flats. But you will meet it one day if you spend any significant time on the water. No other fish soars so far or so gracefully. Once in a great while, one may fall onto your deck. Be sure you return it to the sea.

suggested that one of his boats would make the perfect base camp for any angling adventure I could conceive.

"How about going to the Marquesas?" I asked.

"What are they?"

"Islands just west of Key West."

"A piece of cake," he said. "When do you want the boat down there?"

Four months later, the CEO and I were in Marathon with his top-of-the-line, twin-engine model. Lefty Kreh, Mark Sosin, and Bob Stearns joined us with two Hewes Bonefishers. My brother John, then a history professor at the University of Miami, and his wife were also on hand, although they weren't planning to go to the Marquesas with the rest of us.

The weather forecast for the week was perfect. The only trouble was, the farther the CEO had come from his Midwestern home, the more reluctant he was to take his boat out to sea. That night at dinner, while most of us chatted happily about the pioneering angling we expected to do, the CEO quietly polished off two bottles of wine.

At ten o'clock, on our way back to our rooms, he suddenly announced he was going to take the boat out for a trial run in the dark. Since we couldn't dissuade him, and since I was the trip's organizer, I went along. My brother and sister-in-law came, too. Once we were past the last No Wake sign, the CEO opened her up. As the minutes ticked by, I began to think we might actually get away with it. Then with a sickening lurch that sent us all slamming into the nearest bulkhead, we found ourselves atop a coral shoal.

It took several hours to free the boat. Rather than wait for the rising tide to peak, the CEO told me to wade with the anchor into the darkness of deep water so he could kedge the boat off the bar. By the time we limped back to Marathon, it was evident by the pounding under the hull we had at least one twisted prop shaft. When a mechanic told the CEO that repairs would take a week, he laughed in relief.

My brother and sister-in-law went back to Miami while Bob, Lefty, Mark, and I made the most of the time we had. We wrote no Marquesas stories that spring, but we fattened our files of flats fishing photos, and I got to mess around with barracuda and houndfish again—much to the scorn and amusement of my more sophisticated companions.

Today, jewfish are a protected species. How many did my brothers and I catch and kill? How many of these magnificent groupers with the potential to live more than a century did we sell for three cents a pound uncleaned and five cents a pound cleaned? How many bonefish did we kill for bait? How many permit did we eat? How many of our barracuda ended up on office walls?

Younger readers will condemn us. That's their prerogative and consolation, for angling on the prop-scarred and overfished flats is now a mere scavenging in the ruins of what my brothers and I knew a half century ago. We were participants in the last hurrah of free-for-all angling in the sea. We did what we did because there were relatively few of us, and we couldn't imagine it wouldn't last forever.

Do I feel remorse? Of course, but I don't feel regret. Regret is for things one doesn't do and, as far as I know, we did it all. My brothers and I were fortunate to have been boys in the last great age of innocence and plenty—a time when most Americans still believed there were no limits to their possibilities.

WORLD OF THE SILVER KINGS

Nick Lyons

ow's your heart, Nick?" Jeffrey Cardenas wrote, and sent me a photograph of what a 16-foot hammerhead shark did with one bite to a 150-pound tarpon: There was a head and half of a torso, and a lot of blood on the deck of the Waterlight.

My heart felt pretty good, and not so lost to those pretty little speckled things that I couldn't dream of at least one trip south for the great silver kings. So when an opening broke for two days in prime tarpon time with Jeffrey, I said, "Why not?"

I ordered a 12-weight, 9-foot, 3-inch graphite rod that was very fast and very powerful. Then I traded half a dozen reels I never used for a huge Fin Nor with an intermediate line and six million yards of backing. I bought the strongest sunscreen I could find—to prevent more basal cell carcinomas, which had recently begun to pop out on my forehead like freckles—scrounged sixty or seventy tarpon flies from friends and bought twice as many, and read Lefty and Dimock and all the articles on tarpon I could find in magazines going back ten years. And in the end I wasn't sure I really wanted this kind of fishing at all.

I'd never had a 12-weight rod in my hand; I'd never caught a fish larger than twelve pounds on a fly; and I'd rather gotten to like tiny flies and tough trout lately. Four pounds of such tough trout would be more to my liking, I thought, than these silver monsters I understood not at all.

Still, I'd made the commitment and kept planning hard. I worked out everything with greatest care. I even took a left-handed Fin Nor, though I always reel with my

48

right hand, thinking my right hand could hold the rod better. And day by day the letters came from friends who had tried tarpon fishing: "It's addictive." "You'll give up trout forever." "They're awesome, prehistoric fish!" "I envy you like mad."

Several weeks later I was back home, safe—my rod broken; middle finger of my left hand scarred; bruises on my chest, left arm, and rump; my nose and left arm scaling rudely from the sun; my head awash with dreams of big water and big tarpon. And even now, many weeks later, scores of images keep porpoising in my brain, like great silverbacks rhythmically rising from the sea and falling back.

I see the flats from Miami to Key West as the Jetstream J31 cruises low: so clear and calm I thought they were land, except for the sailboats and skiffs, like skittering caddis, on the flat surface of the thin water.

What a different game it is: standing on the prow of the Waterlight, which dips and rolls in the high winds, line coiled below me—Jeffrey high on the poling platform, eyes peeled to the horizon line, looking for dark purple shapes beneath the surface or silver backs porpoising or nervous water. "One o'clock—about two hundred yards," he calls. "A big school. Large fish. And they're very happy."

I look and see nothing but the thousand refractions of light on the choppy green surface.

"Point your rod to where you think it is."

I point the rod.

"Farther right," he calls—a voice out of the wind, in my ear.

I point the rod to two-thirty. "Farther. Yes. See them?"

I do.

"They're closing quickly. Make sure your line is ready. Keep them in sight. Here they come . . ."

"TROUBLE BREWING" *Peter Corbin*

Thinking back on those two days, I see the giant rays like magic carpets beneath the boat; the sudden appearance of a turtle's head, the size of a grapefruit; a happy tarpon's head out of the water, Cuban anchovies sprouting from its mouth; cormorants working down near the abandoned barge; pelicans diving thunderously; huge nurse sharks mating. Jeffrey says the nurse sharks gather near these islands and sometimes mate as long as twelve hours, twisting and turning together, white belly high, tails thrashing, milt awash in the green seas.

I see Mari making watercolors on the brief sand beach of an island, us rushing from the permit flats as the rain clouds angle toward her.

I see the sheets of rain as we turn tail and race back to Key West, water blasting me from the boat's spray in choppy seas and from above, my eyes stinging from the salt, Mari smiling through it all like a kid on a roller coaster.

I see Jeffrey madly untangling the knot in my fly line, the second day, after the bright forty-pound tarpon took and began to leap with abandon, and Jeffrey untying it and the fish soon coming close under the pressure of the 12-weight and Jeffrey shouting, "If he goes under the boat take it around the front end," and the fish diving under, me following stupidly with the rod, the new 12-weight busting cleanly with a bang, Jeffrey leaping to get the tip section that came free when the fish was off, me seeing that photograph he'd sent me of half a tarpon, and then Jeffrey hoisting himself back on board and all of us laughing.

It was very different for me out on the flats. I saw and understood too little. I felt untutored for it. In that one moment when tarpon and poled boat began to intersect, I had moments to get my line in the air, double-haul, and place it quickly in the line of the huge fish. I got one cast, perhaps two. I got buck fever and crashed key casts, after Jeffrey had spent twenty minutes poling into position. I nearly put a fly into his neck

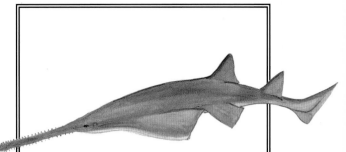

SMALLTOOTH SAWFISH
Pristis pectinatus

If you are fortunate enough to see the rare smalltooth sawfish, you will never forget it. Sawfish are large (up to twenty feet long) sharklike rays that slash their tooth-edged "sawbill" through schools of baitfish. They are docile, which has almost cost them their survival. One or two are spotted in the Marquesas each year.

when I cast at twelve o'clock. I cast too fast. I cast late. I forgot everything I'd read, everything I'd been told, everything I'd practiced the day before in a skiff in the backcountry with a friend. After we'd fished the backcountry and practiced with the big 12-weight, I tripped getting out of the boat—nervous before I was within thirty miles of tarpon—and smashed my chest, my left arm, and my rump. Out on the flats I forgot the sunscreen I'd bought and only used the one fly that Jeffrey gave me.

I took a tarpon on my first cast the second day, jumped another, cast poorly much of the time, decently on occasion, and half began to think I understood something (though I didn't), and I wondered if I could ever master this exhilarating sport.

The two days had started with a minute of high drama, and I may even have thought then that I understood a bit more than I could possibly understand.

We had no sooner arrived on the flats the first day than Jeffrey tied on a fly with a bright red head that had been hot the past week. He said to keep alert. I remember a sailfish captain telling me that a dozen years earlier, and my sitting in the big fighting chair for five hours—highly alert, dragging a rigged bait fruitlessly.

Not this time. Two minutes after we arrived, Jeffrey spotted silverbacks, not eighty feet away. You couldn't miss them. My legs turned to jelly. But I stripped out line, stepped onto the casting area, saw the ruffled water angling to us, and seconds later they were at eleven o'clock, forty-five feet off to the left, and closing.

For three weeks I have been trying to get a truly clear picture of what happened next. All is awash in silver and confusion.

Seconds after I made my first cast ever to a tarpon, a huge fish—over one hundred pounds—took the fly. I struck three or four times hard (as I'd been instructed); the fish careened dead away from the boat and leapt once, thunderously, rising like some great silver missile, shaking, vibrating in the air, and then crashing back into the sea.

It was off the hook.

There were voices behind me, but my first thought was that I might get in another cast before this large school passed. The line was too far out to put it in the air, so I began to strip it—fishing it, as I always do when fish are near.

Another tarpon picked up the fly. I felt the sudden surge of power, reared back three or four times, and this time the fish was on. Up it went—bright silver and electric, quivering with life—and I bowed (or at least leaned enough) and the fish stayed hooked.

There is an old 1920s cartoon about a Mississippi fisherman hooked up to a truly gigantic catfish, with the legend: "Fish, do I have you or do you have me?" With my tarpon I could not tell. The fish took line when it suited him; it leapt magnificently; at times it felt unbudgeable. It proved to be of modest size—about seventy-five pounds—but it was more than enough fish for the likes of me, and while I fought it, Jeffrey taught me how to gain line, keep the fish from rolling, apply maximum pressure, and haul opposite the tug of the fish. Reeling hard with my unused left hand, I put a huge welt on my middle finger; I could barely lift my right arm.

An hour later the fish turned sideways and the fight neared its end.

Those two days—my first on the flats—haunt me. My heart held—but I lost a piece of it to the world of the silver kings.

My Transformational Day

Calvin Trillin

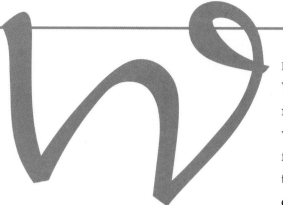

HEN I WENT FLATS FISHING NEAR KEY West with John Cole, I thought we might get into a disagreement about whether we were going to release the fish we caught. John is a fish releaser of the first order. I, on the other hand, consider that sort of thing contrary to the laws of nature. I'm going to stop eating any fish I catch when the lions of East Africa officially adopt a catch-and-release policy on wildebeests.

Even though I hadn't had much fishing experience, I knew that it would make sense to establish a policy on catch-and-release before we landed the first fish: holding that discussion with the fish flopping around on the bottom of the boat sort of puts pressure on one side. But I hadn't been able to bring up the subject with John. He was too busy being rhapsodic about the experience we were having on the flats.

He kept saying, "You are now among the fortunate anglers who have fished the thin waters from the Contents to Cottrell, and west of Key West to the Marquesas," or words to that effect.

I didn't want to seem ungrateful for the privilege, but I was beginning to notice that we hadn't had any bites. "I think I'd feel even more fortunate if I caught a fish, John," I said in reply.

"Are you taking in the wonder and luminosity of the flats themselves?" John said.

"So far, that's about all I've taken in," I said.

About an hour into the trip, John seemed to take a break in his talk about the transformational quality of flats fishing. I guess he ran out of adjectives.

I realized that this would be a good time to bring up the catch-and-release question. But it seemed so mundane compared to luminosity and all that. I kept quiet, and worried that we might have to hold that discussion in front of a flopping fish after all. I needn't have worried. We didn't catch any fish. We didn't get a nibble. Zip. A shutout.

John said that he was disappointed that I didn't experience the thrill of having a bonefish on the line. I was actually sort of relieved. A bonefish didn't sound like the sort of thing I'd look forward to picking my way through just to keep my spot in the food chain secure.

"As you know, this location, at the meeting place of the Gulf and the Atlantic, is unique," John said, as we got

BLACK SKIMMER

Rynchops niger

On winter days in Key West, flocks of black skimmers gather at the end of lonely wharves with their faces into the wind. When the winds calm, they fish, dipping their longer lower bills into the water's surface as they fly just above it. No other bird in the world fishes or looks like the skimmer.

to the dock. "These shoal waters are among the finest saltwater sports fishing resources in the world."

"I guess we could be considered good citizens, then," I said. "We managed to restrain ourselves from depleting the resources in the slightest."

We gathered up our gear. I told John I'd buy him a beer if he promised not to say anything else about luminosity. He accepted.

Ghosts in the Storm

Robert F. Jones

IT WAS WEIRD OUT THAT NIGHT, WEIRD LIKE HUMMING, RIGHT FROM THE start. You could kind of feel her humming out there, spinning clockwise to the north and a bit east, a long way off it felt, but then Eddie Kilrain came in the door, an old-timer right off the plane, dressed in his baggy shorts and that faded blue and green aloha shirt from ten or twelve years ago, pale as a milkshake from a winter up north, and came walking over to me at the bar in Captain Tony's.

He said to me, "Give me a . . ."

And a Conch wannabe next to him at the bar to his left, a big guy who'd been drinking when I came in, looked down at Eddie all red-eyed and said in a loud, thick voice, "Whattaya, a fag? No faggots allowed here, sister."

"Give me a piña colada, please," Eddie said to the bartender. He lisped a bit, for effect, and I knew what was coming. Then he turned toward the wannabe, smiled shyly, and faked a right, just the beginnings of a puny little girl-throw right, and as the wannabe's hands came up Eddie brought his left across in a short, tight screwball punch that took the wannabe wrist deep right over the liver, and as the wannabe folded toward him Eddie caught the wannabe by the throat with his other hand and held him there, hanging, and he says to him, "That's a little trick I know, it's called the Trick of the Ga Bolga. That's where you fuck yourself right up the ass. You're a rude son of a bitch, and I have it in mind to teach you a few more tricks. Now get outta here."

Eddie Kilrain spun him around and hitched up the wannabe's shorts in a wedgie and frog-marched him quick to the door.

OSPREY
Pandion haliaetus

The only hawk that feeds exclusively on fish, the osprey has a wingspan that reaches six feet. With those wings folded, the osprey drops like a missile from the sky and submerges for a moment as its talons close on a mullet or houndfish. Their stick nests top many Keys channel markers.

The wannabe was out of there.

"The weather doesn't feel good," Eddie said to me.

"I think it's moving north," I said. "Of course it could swing back."

The last time we'd fished together was six years ago anyway, but that's Eddie's style, every time I see him it's like we fished yesterday.

"I shouldn't've come down," he said. The bartender brought him his drink. It was a great big piña colada, like a triple. Eddie Kilrain looked at it and poured it on the floor.

"Give me a Jack this time," he said, "about yay big. No ice."

"You got it," the bartender said.

"Listen," Eddie Kilrain said to me. "I shouldn't've come down here. The weather is moody and this whole town's fucked up. Who was that asshole? When I flew in, all I could see was wheel tracks, all over the flats from Largo on down. What the hell is it with all this high-rise?"

"It's a whole new town," I told him. "Hey, it's a whole new crowd down here now, a whole lot of new types of guys fishing, women too, and lots more guides, but the fish are still here. The weather? Well, this time of year you never know."

He looked at me hard.

"Eddie," I told him, "if we get blown out, it won't cost you nothing."

He looked at me even harder.

He turned toward the bar and swallowed his Jack. "So how the hell are you, Cap?" he said.

The weather was still screwy the next morning when he met me at Garrison Bight. He carried his three canvas rod cases, as usual, the #12 Sage already rigged for tarpon, a #9 for permit or bone or mutton, and if things were really slow, that dinky little cat's whisker of a #5 that he likes for little cuda in among the mangroves knees.

He was still wearing the shorts and aloha shirt, no hat, and he was still pale as a pork belly. I looked up at the sky. Clear overhead and to the west, but up to the north there were big anvils showing blue-black with white teeth in them. Little mare's tails of cirrus curled out above the anvils and snaked their way southwest.

"You're going to get burnt to a crisp," I told him. "Even if it clouds up later, which it looks like it's making to do."

"Ta da," he said, and fished a big plastic bottle of SPF 45 sunblock from his hip pocket. He threw it down in the skiff.

We ran out past Tank Island along the buoyed channel, then west through the Lakes passage. There was no wind at all and the water looked like grease in a fry pan getting ready to boil. No wind at all but the apparent wind at forty knots as we raced out past Mule and Archer, Crawfish, and the Mullets, on past Cottrell and Man and Ballast and Woman Keys until we got abeam of Boca Grande, where I shut her down to an idle. Boca Grande Channel lay ahead of us, smooth as the interstate. You hardly ever see it that way.

Eddie Kilrain said, "The Marquesas, driver, and step on it." He was smearing himself all over with sunblock, and he had little white squiggles on his face where he hadn't rubbed it in yet, under his eyes like an albino raccoon.

"It's a long run," I said. "And I don't like this weather one bit. Too damn calm. That means it's going to blow like a bastard sometime today."

"I want those tarpon," he said. "Those tarpon in the south channel. Those big mammies, Cap. They ought to be running about now."

"Hey," I said. "It's just your first day out. You don't want to overdo it, Ed. That sunblock bottle could read SPF 1000 but you'd burn up anyway. Hell, you could be fishing neck deep in a vat of it, you'd still burn up, white as you are. Remember that time at Homosassa?"

One year he'd come down from New York to Homosassa. I'd trailered the skiff up there to fish the big tarpon that come in there in June, looking for that two-hundred-pounder that nobody's caught yet, and he'd sunburned so bad we had to put him in the hospital.

He still had sun warts all over him, and I could see them raising their little watery heads even under all that gunk he'd just smeared on.

"I want them tarpon at the Marquesas," he said. He stuck out his lower lip like a stubborn kid about to cry for a lollipop. "And don't you Homosassa me, Cap. As for remembering, you might perhaps recall who put up the money for this shitbucket."

She's a sixteen-foot Dolphin Super Skiff with a fifty-five-horse Evinrude, a light riding beauty without any slap to her, an easy poler, and Eddie Kilrain bought her for me when he sunk my Maverick Mirage and both of us with her because I'd been damn fool enough to let him take the wheel one time and he tore her guts out at speed on a coral head a blind man could have seen a mile away. But he was right. The boat he was riding in was the boat he'd bought me.

We headed out west for the Marquesas. I have to admit there is something magnetic about that place, the low, marly mangrove hummocks, the sunlight glinting off the needles of the pines on the bigger islands, ospreys and frigatebirds swinging high over the offshore combers waiting to rob the sea of its fish. Maybe a big hammerhead or two cruising the flats real slow, bellies brushing the turtle grass, the water bulging weirdly when they put on a burst of speed. And nobody else in sight, usually, not another boat or another angler, only a shrimper maybe, heading in to Cayo Hueso, one guy maybe leaning on the rail lonelylike, watching us stake off near the pass, waiting for tarpon to roll. Wondering what it's like to be rich and fish just for fun. Real quiet, the Marquesas.

JEFFREY CARDENAS

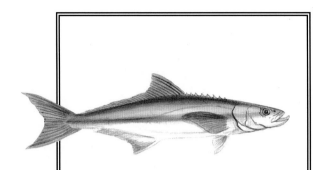

COBIA
Rachycentron canadus

Often a dark brown shadow that may be an imposing three or four feet long will make a pass at a fly or lure. If identification is a guess at best, most anglers will say "cobia" and will not often be disproved. An infrequent flats visitor, this roving predator turns up more often in mangrove sloughs and is a rousing fighter.

Not today, though. By the time we got there the seas were running all cockeyed, every which way. No wind yet, but an odd light hung over the place, the birds all up and frantic; we could hear them screaming and see the depth-charge bursts of diving pelicans from a full mile off. Great glassy swells rolled sloshing through the channel from wall to mangrove wall when we got there, tall as a man from trough to crest, and looking down through the tilting water we could see tarpon rolling through nonstop like a train of silver-blue freight cars over the turtle grass. Before I'd even staked her off Eddie Kilrain grabbed the big Sage, stripped off about fifty feet of fly line, false-cast once or twice, and was into a fish before the big, bright purple-and-orange Harry Kime fly had sunk two feet. *Ba-wham*, like that.

The tarpon peeled out of the Silver King Express and shot into the sky, his gill plates rattling like a burst from an Uzi, and *bam*, he was back down in the water and then back up again, hanging even higher against the sky this time, upside down in a halo of pulverized water. Eddie let him jump six or eight times, long greyhounding jumps to the southeast, then pointed the rod tip at him, palmed in some drag, and broke him off on purpose. He tied on another fly.

You don't want to let them jump their hearts out, do you? You're going to release them anyhow, aren't you? While they're all here and running, why not hook a few more? The real excitement with tarpon is the take and the first few jumps. After that, it's just hard work. At any rate, that was Eddie Kilrain's philosophy.

Eddie jumped two more, eighty-pounders or so like that first one, and on the third tarpon the wind hit us. Only a puff at first, a warning slap, but it took me by surprise. I'd been watching the action, leaning on the push pole, not paying attention to the weather. Now I looked to the northeast, and there was a squall bearing down on us a mile a minute. I barely had time to get the engine cranking and the skiff turned around into the teeth of it when the wind hit full force—hard, pelting rain so thick it was tough to breathe, coming near horizontal on the wind. The sea stood up quick on the shoal ground, green and white and bitter in our eyes. I ran her out into it away from the shallows. The mangroves were just waiting in there to snag us. It was over in minutes, loud ones, wet ones, but that was just a taste of what was coming.

Behind the first squall line stood a much taller, darker wall of weather, with lightning in its belly. It reached from horizon to horizon, the whole northeast-to-southeast sky black as doom, you couldn't see the top, and the thunder growled like an artillery bombardment clear back to Cayo Hueso. There was no way out of it, not through this shit. I secured the push pole and ran her out fast toward the Quicksands, hoping to reach the deep channel before the main storm hit. It was that or duck around into the lee to the northwest of the Marquesas, but there was too much shoal water that way and we'd be running broadside to the seas—Swamp City for certain sure. A wind like that could flip you like a flapjack.

"What do you think?" Eddie yelled.

"I'm going to run for Fort Jeff," I yelled back. "Redline all the way. We'll have following seas, a following wind, and if she don't broach to we'll be all right in the boat basin on Garden Key. We can cumshaw some gas from another boat when we get there."

"Your call, Captain," Eddie said doubtfully. But he grinned, grabbed the bow painter, and stood there facing forward with his legs braced.

It was the wildest, wettest roller-coaster ride I've ever been on. The seas got taller, steeper and steeper. At the top of the crests we'd be armpit deep in spume whipped off the crest by the howling wind, pumps working like fire hoses, then we'd swoop down into the trough like on a surfboard, me gunning her to the max so that comber behind us couldn't catch up and clip us sideways, then run like in slow motion, it felt, but still at the redline up to the top of the next crest—but I don't know, maybe we only rode the same two waves all the way to Fort Jefferson. I nearly lost her a couple of times when the wind hooked around below a raggedy peak to the right or the left and hit us with a corkscrew punch like that little liver hook Eddie'd stopped the wannabe with. Eddie got knocked off his feet a few times, slewed sideways by the twisting, jumping dance of the little Dolphin, but the skiff really seemed to love it all, she was in her element—she wants to be a surfboard I guess. Me and Eddie were both pretty arm-weary by the time we raised Fort Jeff.

We cut around the backside and into the boat basin, the old six-sided red brick fort rising grim and gaunt against the wild skies. The gas tanks ran dry just as we kissed the seawall. There were no other boats in the basin.

After the storm blew through we climbed up on the parapets. As far as we could see in any direction, the great, crashing waves were exploding as they met, what they call a confusion of currents. The fort shook when the waves hit the seawall. I heard a few bricks fall from the crumbling walls and shatter on the parade ground below. I could hear the ghosts in the storm still muttering off to the southwest. We might have been muttering with them. A few gulls circled over the surf line, looking for dead fish, and high overhead in the dirty red sunset light I could see the frigatebirds wheeling. Robbers, all of us. The air was as wet as a soggy T-shirt.

"Dry Tortugas, my ass," Eddie Kilrain said. "Well, Cap, I guess we're prisoners here for a while. Just like Doctor Mudd and all those hard cases they used to send here in the old days. It's pitiful."

"At least till the next boat shows," I said. "But there's still plenty of drinking water in the jugs, all this rainwater pooled in the fort if it comes to that. We never ate our sandwiches for lunch, and anyway we can always catch fish."

Eddie laughed. He looked down at the sun boils on his arms. His face was as red

"THE YELLOW SKIFF" *Peter Corbin*

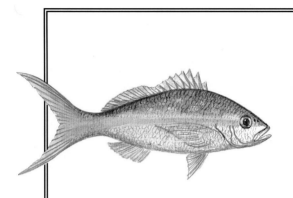

Yellowtail Snapper

Ocyurus chrysurus

Not often seen on the flats, yellowtail are more at home on the reefs, where they can be chummed to the surface and taken on a fly, lure, or baited hook. A lovely, firm-fleshed, dramatic fish, the yellowtail is a dining staple in the Keys, very likely to turn up on restaurant menus.

as the fort itself. He was shivering a bit, humming to himself, hurting, but he wouldn't let it show.

"I haven't been out here in twenty years," Eddie said quietly, maybe with a touch of wonder in his voice. "You ever hear of a Key West captain named . . . Let's call him Grandee Mercer. A short, pussel-gutted, slab-faced, sneaky-eyed Cajun? No, you're too young.

"This guy could cook like Paul Prudhomme, though, and he hadn't been a bad fisherman once upon a time. He'd always been truculent—you know how those old-time skippers were—but then he got into the booze, big time, and went from surly to downright mean. The low point came when he raped a girl with a broken-off swab handle.

"I was still fishing big game on the blue water back in those days, hadn't gotten into the fly rod yet. We came out here with Mercer for wahoo, cobia, amberjack, and big barracuda. He'd just quit drinking—doctor told him he'd be dead in a month if he continued—and he was meaner than a gut-shot coyote, especially when he caught us popping a beer or two. Nothing but bitch and sulk and insult from the time we left Cayo Hueso, everything we did was wrong, until finally one evening we came up here on the parapets for a council of war. Five more days of this? No way. It was a night just like this one. Sitting up here in the cold, bleak sunset among the ghosts and the rusting cannons, it was like back in the days when this was a pirates' roost. Half facetiously, I proposed killing Mercer—on the run to the Tortugas we'd come through heavy weather like today, and we could just say he'd gone overboard during the storm. But two of the guys on the trip were lawyers, and they counseled against it. Instead we went back to the boat and told Mercer to cut the trip short, head back to Key West the next morning. We'd paid him his full price anyway. He called us pussies but finally agreed.

"Next day we stopped at the wreck of the *Val Banera* on the way back in to chum up some mutton snapper for Mercer to sell—'Mutton's better'n nuttin',' he always said. One of the guys on the trip was an old navy buddy of mine, a big, clumsy, gentle guy who was embroiled in a messy divorce at the time, and he couldn't land a fish to save his soul—just kept breaking them off or losing them at the boat by giving them too much slack. Mercer turned on him that morning, called him all kinds of obscenities. Then he slapped my friend across the face. At that moment my eye fell on the lead-cored shark billy. I grabbed it when Mercer's back was turned, hefted it. Zeroed in on the back of his fat, greasy-haired skull. One of the lawyers saw what I was up to and grabbed my arm. He said real serious, 'Don't do it, Ed.' "

Eddie Kilrain paused, then cleared his throat.

"But I did it," he said softly. "All planned and executed in a red-eyed instant, and no bastard ever deserved to die more than Mercer."

He lowered his head and shook it from side to side, wondering.

"Well, it got ugly then," Eddie said. "We emptied him out like you would a big tuna—took him over the side for that so we'd have less blood on the deck—we loaded his belly with ballast from the bilges. We laced him up from the fish line, used a rusty old fid to punch the holes, and sunk him out there in the Quicksands, down with all those bodies in the wreck of the *Val Banera*."

He laughed again, short and bitter.

He said, "The lawyers didn't watch that part. They were busy preparing our alibi. Lawyers are good at that."

I'd heard of the *Val Banera*. She was a Spanish liner that went aground and foundered off the Marquesas back in 1919 with five hundred souls aboard. I think Hemingway wrote about her in one of his stories.

We sat there watching the sunset.

"You don't know what to make of it, do you, Cap?" he said. "Men bit by the sun talk crazy." He smiled. "But you know, Cap, I'm still paying the price. Think of it. We're prisoners of this place no matter what happens. All of it, from Garrison Bight to Fort Jeff. Once you've fished your way out here you're in it for keeps. You're a damn fool lifer. As long as the tarpon are running we'll still be out here, hey? Or guys like us, anyways. But what the hell, it's a life term worth serving."

Something splashed down there in the boat basin, a sound smaller but more insistent than the grumbling of the sea. We looked down. Then another one rolled near the harbor mouth, that dull silver flash, then another flash right behind it; they were daisy-chaining inside the seawall. Eddie Kilrain got up and ran for the staircase, ran for the skiff, ran for his fly rod.

There were tarpon down there, corralled by the storm.

A WORLD-RECORD DINNER
from AN OUTSIDE CHANCE

Thomas McGuane

I CONCEDE THAT "MUTTON SNAPPER" IS HARDLY A PREPOSSESSING TITLE. The sheep, from which the name derives, is not much of an animal. No civilized person deals with him except in chops and stews. To bleat is not to sing out in a commanding baritone; to be sheepish is scarcely to possess a virtue for which civilization rolls out its more impressive carpets.

And it is true that the fish, as you may have suspected, is not at all handsome, with its large and vacant-looking head, crazy red eye, and haphazard black spot just shy of its tail. Yet its brick-orange flanks and red tail are rather tropical and fine, and for a number of reasons it deserves consideration as major light-tackle game. When you have been incessantly outwitted by the mutton snapper, you cease to emphasize his vaguely doltish exterior.

To begin with, mutton snappers share with the most pursued shallow-water game fish a combination of hair-trigger perceptions. They are wild and spooky, difficult to deceive, and very powerful. Taken under optimum conditions, they are as enthralling as any species that haunts the flats.

Like most flats fish, the mutton snapper is primarily a creature of deep water, another individual thread in the ocean system that, following its own particular necessity, crisscrosses the lives and functions of the animals that share its habitat. Which is to say that in looking for one fish you find another—and maybe in the end you find it all.

After a long winter's flats fishing, I had naturally acquired a ready facility for recognizing most anything that came along. A flat is a circumscribed habitat so far as

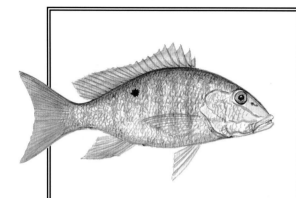

MUTTON SNAPPER

Lutjanus analis

Spectacularly colored with oranges and silver, the mutton snapper often swims in the cloudy wake of feeding rays, waiting for crabs and shrimp fleeing the larger fish. Reaching twenty pounds or more, the mutton is a fly caster's prize, both on the line and on the plate. So few are left, however, that a quick release is best.

larger fish are concerned. The first mutton snappers I found were encountered while I was poling for permit on flood tides close to the keys. They were wild fish, hustling around in their curious way and pushing abrupt knuckles of wake in the thin water. Their red tails made them unmistakable.

They seemed so conscious of the skiff that it was hard to see how they might be taken on a fly rod. Besides, they were hard to find, somewhat harder, for example, than permit, and they were every bit as alert and quick to flush.

Last May, Guy de la Valdene and I began to fish for them in earnest, spurred on from time to time by the sight of brilliant red forks in the air. The fish often seemed hurried, and when we would pole to the place where we had seen a tail, there would be nothing. Most of the first fish we found were in a grassy basin south of Key West, a shallow place usually good for a few shots at permit. The basin was little more than a declivity in the long-running ocean bank that reaches from just below Key West to the Boca Grande Channel—and across which lie the Marquesas.

Early one hot day Guy and I began to fish this basin. A long convection buildup of clouds lay along the spine of the keys, like a mirror image of the islands themselves, all the way to Boca Grande, and then scattered in cottony streamers to the west. So we fished in a shadow most of the day, straining to find fish in the turtle grass.

With the leisurely wan hope that comes of being on a flat at no particular tide, I was poling the skiff. We passed a small depression on the flat and suddenly spotted two mutton snappers floating close to the bottom with the antsy, fidgeting look they so often have. Guy made an excellent cast and a fish responded immediately. My hopes sank as it overtook and began to follow the fly with the kind of examining pursuit we had come to associate with one of the permit's more refined refusals. But, with considerable élan, Guy stopped the fly and let it sink to the bottom. The snapper paused behind the fly at a slight forward tilt and then, in what is to the flats fisherman a thrilling gesture, he tilted over onto his head and tailed, the great, actually wondrous, fork in the air, precisely marking the position of Guy's fly.

I looked toward the stern. Guy was poised, line still slack, rod tip down. He gave the fish three full seconds and I watched him lift the rod, feeling foredoomed that the line would glide back slack. But the rod bowed in a clean gesture toward the fly line, which was inscribed from rod tip to still tailing fish. Abruptly, the fish was level in the water again and surging away from us in a globe of wake that it pushed before itself; a thin sheet of water stood behind the leader as it sheared the surface.

The first long run ended with the fly pulling free. The childish gloom of sport descended. As Guy reeled in his line and backing, I let the boat drift in on the tide toward the little community of stilt houses standing mysteriously in spiderlike shadows off Boca Grande Key. Nearby, an old sail-powered commercial boat rusted on the bank that claimed it, a long row of black cormorants on its crumbling iron rail.

"Well," said Guy, "I guess they'll take the fly."

It was late in the afternoon and Guy was still poling. I stood in the gun seat, as we had come to call the aft casting platform, trailing my loop of fly line. We were zigzagging around in our grassy basin, fishing out the last of the incoming tide and getting shots from time to time at permit. From directly out of the light, a large stingray was swimming toward us, and in front of it were two large fish, indistinguishably back-lit. Because they were with the ray, these were necessarily feeding fish. I had time to roll my trailing loop into the air, make a quick false cast, then throw. The left-hand fish, facing me, veered off and struck. I had him briefly, but long enough to feel an almost implacable power, enough to burn a finger freeing loose fly line. Since mutton snappers frequently came into this basin from deep water with rays, we presumed that is what had taken my fly.

Whatever, it joined that throng of shades, touched and unseen, that haunt the angler—fish felt and lost, big ones that got away that are the subject of levity to nonanglers but of a deeper emotion to the angler himself.

Rays are a common sight on the flats. The game fish seldom follow the pretty spotted eagle rays, which have a perfection of shape and movement that is beyond quick description. They are dark and beautifully spotted like a fawn or leopard; as a wing is lifted to propel them the exquisite, creamy ventral surfaces are exposed. Spotted eagle rays mud less than stingrays; their oval mouths seem made for more exact procedures. When the boat is upon them they flush with long perfect sweeps of their wings, and when they are lost to the eye the swirls and turbulence of their deceptively powerful movements continue to disturb the surface.

The platitudinous stingray with his torpid, carpetlike movements, on the other hand, holds some special interest for game fish. Jacks, snappers, and permit will follow a feeding stingray throughout the tide, using the ray as a kind of stalking horse to scare up small fish and crabs. When a fish is found accompanying a ray, it may be assumed that he is feeding rather than traveling. A suitable presentation must be made.

We knew where we could find rays. We often saw them on the soft backsides of banks whose harder edges we fished for permit. We had a grandly complex set of banks that stretched from the Atlantic to the Gulf of Mexico; we had laboriously laid out its tortuous inner channels and developed some sense of the sequence in which permit used its individual flats and banks. But always we had fished the edges.

Today we wanted to go into the interior of the banks on incoming water and fish well up on the soft bottom. We made the long run from Key West in the early morning, the scattered keys looking deep, wet, and green on the slate sea. We passed Mule,

Archer, Big and Little Mullet, Cottrell, Barracuda, Man, Woman, Ballast, and Boca Grande, on out past the iron marker, west into the first gut.

The flat was dotted with luminous slicks of mudding rays. Guy took the pole and we tracked down the rays one by one, finding them mainly alone, but here and there seeing the fleeting red forks or discovering the nervous snappers too late.

Eventually we found a single large snapper working a stingray. The ray was making such an extensive mud that it seemed unlikely the snapper could find a retrieved fly. In any case, the excitement of watching the tailing fish collaborate with the ray and the measuring in my mind's eye of the breadth of that fork went a long way toward totally eroding my composure.

The mutton snapper was tailing when I cast, and I threw well beyond the ray and retrieved the large fly through the edge of the slick. The tail dropped abruptly, and my first thought was that I had flushed the snapper. Then I saw the wake directly behind my fly and knew I was getting a follow. I hoped for a take straightaway but none came. I had to stop the fly and let it go to the bottom, an act that has always felt entirely unnatural to me. The fish tipped up instantly, tail entirely out of the water. I lifted the rod tentatively and with terror, then I came up tight and the fish was running.

Water streamed up the leader with a silky shearing noise, and the snapper peeled off in a bulge of water tinted by his own brick-red hue. The flat was a broad one and the snapper failed to clear it to deep water on his first run. At the end of that run he turned perpendicular to the line and held there for a while, implacable as a fire hydrant. Then, with an air of having made the decision himself, he allowed me to retrieve him at his own sullen rate. I began to look around for the net but found Guy one step ahead of me, the big net at parade rest.

SOUTHERN STINGRAY

Dasyatis americana

A dark flat fish as much as five feet wide with a long, mean-looking tail, stingrays like to burrow in the marl, hiding themselves under a layer of sand. When you wade the flats, shuffle your feet, don't pick them up. If you step on a stingray, you're likely to get stung, and it hurts like hell.

My glances for the net were optimistic ones. There were a number of runs to be endured. With a fish badly wanted, it is always simple to imagine the hook pulling free, the leader breaking, the dead feeling in the slack rod. Five minutes later the fish was at the boat, succinctly netted by Guy.

It seemed quite big, bigger than I expected. A short time after landing the fish we ran into a local guide who weighed it: a little over 15 pounds, the world record on a fly.

That night the world record was dispatched as follows: deprived of head and innards, he was stuffed with shrimp, shallots, buttered crumbs, parsley, tarragon, and mushrooms, then rinsed down the gullets of hungry anglers with gouts of cold domestic Chablis. I would wish a similar fate upon all world records that are not released at the boat.

The next day Guy took another big fish, this one 13 pounds, and we began to feel we were getting the hang of it. This fish was given to a Cuban friend at the yard who remembered mutton snappers in the Havana markets. He carried Guy's fish around in a formal march, under the stored hulls, through the dry shed, and out to the carpenter's shop, before giving it the place of honor on the front seat of his pickup.

When we looked for the snappers in the next few days we could not find them. The rays came in on the same tides, but now they were alone. A week or so later the commercial fisherman found the snappers on the 120-foot contour offshore, 118 feet out of our depth. But we had had our glimpse and knew we would be waiting for them next spring on the flats.

Best Friends

John Cole

OU HAVE TO UNDERSTAND: I WENT TO KEY WEST FOR THE fishing. I'd been waiting almost sixty years for the chance, ever since our mother towed my younger brother and me off to the Metropolitan Museum. Like the afternoon concerts at Carnegie Hall, visits to art galleries on 57th Street, and assigned readings of the classics, time spent in front of the Metropolitan's paintings was one more assurance that Helen Cole's two oldest sons would acquire a substantial spine of cultural sophistication before their adolescence ended.

Most of the process was painless, some of it enjoyable. But my first look at Winslow Homer's Caribbean watercolors was unforgettable. Somewhere in the turquoise blues and aquamarine greens, there in those sweeping spaces of sea and sky, I could see myself as a man. There was where I would be; I knew that. There with those palm fronds fluttering under clouds the color of silver milk, there where shark shadows glowed just under the surface of a shining sea and where a small boat floated to freedom in a place where the sun was forever unsullied by city smoke. That's where I would be.

But I had to wait until my sixty-third year before I got the chance. By then it was almost too late; I was not properly equipped for a journey south. The treasury was barren, and there was little or no hope that a move to Key West would replenish it.

Still, with those Homer visions breaking like tidal waves across my dreams, we went anyway, Jean and I, packed up, roots yanked clear, and friends and family left in

NEEDLEFISH

Scomberesox saurus

Smaller than the houndfish and not as much of a leaper, the needlefish spends its days close to the surface, so you are likely to see it almost anywhere in the waters off the Keys. It is a favorite dish of all predators, including the barracuda, which is why it spends most of those days swimming and leaping for its life.

the rubble of our departure. I arrived in Key West to take a job in an enterprise with the shelf life of an open oyster.

But there was the Gulf, and there, by God, were those milky clouds and that turquoise sea. And there were more long and lonely reaches of pale shoals than even Homer's genius had promised me. Fish by the tens of thousands traveled those shoals, fluttering like flowers above sea beds swept by gentle tides. Every morning, every noon, and as late as midnight I had only to stroll a few steps to any of the docks and piers that ringed that small island city and I would see fish. Great tarpon turned under the lights of nights so sultry I wished for gills. Needlefish and mullet flashed in the forenoon sunlight, so close I could touch them if I were quick enough. And there, always, day and night, night and day, the still presence of great barracuda hovered, their menace withheld, apparently asleep. Their dark shapes greeted me everywhere, and I began to love them.

Even without a job, and at times perilously close to being without a home, I managed to keep a boat of some sort for each of those eight years in Key West. Small boats, each of them, none larger than sixteen feet. None of them new, each of them needing critical repairs, some of them teetering on the brink of unacceptable risk. But all of them capable of carrying me across those bright waters and through those gardens of fish.

When you can fish every day, and in Key West you can, you must learn to fish alone. There are very few men obsessed, and even fewer who can accommodate their obsession. There were none, I discovered, regularly capable of accommodating mine. So I modified my equipment to meet the demands of my need to fish the flats.

I carried a sea anchor aboard, its line fast to a stern cleat. When I had judged the confluences of wind and tidal currents that fanned the flat I wanted to fish, I would shut down the outboard, swivel its lower unit up above the waterline, and begin a drift calculated to take me across the flat's most promising acres. The sea anchor regulated drift speed: If I wanted to go slower, I gave the funnel-shaped drag more scope; if I needed less of a brake, I shortened the line until the resistance astern did little but keep the bow headed downwind.

Drifting thus without a sound, I approached fish more silently than even the finest flats skiff poled by the most accomplished guide. I did not pole. I stood amidships with my hands on my oars, and used those oars to change direction when I spotted a fish I could cast to. When I drifted into casting range, I gently shipped the oars, stepped up onto the bow platform, and began my false casts with line that had already been stripped.

That's how it worked, really. But how everything behaved is what counted. Often, too often, my casts would be off target. Other times, the fish would spook. And then there were all those moments I'd rather not discuss: times when I had my feet firmly atop my fly line; times when the wind would catch the fly and slam it happily into my shoulder blades; and times when I would strip the fly directly into a pod of floating weed instead of across the nose of an inquisitive fish.

But I was there under the sky, afloat on the sky's reflections, looking into sunlight beneath my bow. I was there alone, just a few miles from a city but nevertheless in places where I could lose my solitary self in a water wilderness of sinuous channels and brooding mangrove hummocks. And everywhere, I met fish. Great eagle rays and leopard rays flew with such majestic and unhurried aplomb that I never failed to pause and watch as if they were a passing parade. Houndfish and needlefish embroidered frothy stitches as they hurdled, always in a panic, leaving the water as soon as they touched it as if the air above was where they sought to swim.

Nurse sharks, bonnethead, blacktip, and lemon sharks, each curled and glided into and out of my ken, some of them large enough to keep me silent where I stood,

LEMON SHARK

Negaprion brevirostris

Lovely when it "lights up" in pursuit of its dinner, the lemon shark is a slim, yellow-brown shark with a large dorsal and graceful moves. They will eat flies and attack plugs, and are themselves tasty when small and steaked. As long as eleven feet, they are seen often on the flats.

fearful for a moment of slipping overboard. And there were times when tarpon surfaced before me, their silver shoulders rising from the sea, their huge black eyes staring at my presumptuous self, setting me to trembling as I tried to put a fly in front of their procession. Once or twice, I did, and there was short-lived chaos as a great fish jumped and hung there on my memory's screen long enough for immortality in the pages of my fishing history.

Several times I saw permit, their pewter sides rolling like silver wheels along a flat's edge, weaving out of a channel's deeper blue into the revealing light along the shoal. They were always gone by the time I had recovered from astonishment and cast into the shadows where they had just been.

It was barracuda that I saw most often, almost every day. And it was barracuda that allowed me to live so much of the dream I had been nurturing all those years.

In those waters, from the Contents west to the Marquesas and beyond, barracuda are ubiquitous. And through the colder months (cold for Key West is 68 degrees), great oceanic barracuda stroll in from the chilling Atlantic and take their places on the Gulf-side flats, in the thin water that responds to even a winter sun. Sometimes after a still and chilly night I would come upon thirty or forty barracuda lounging in a kind of alert paralysis on a single, small stretch of pale flats covered by less than two feet of clear water. It was, of course, too much of a convocation to be worked with a fly. Even the most delicate presentation would trip some watchdog's sensor, and the entire school would galvanize in a sibilant rush of turbulence and rocket off this way and that: gone in a fraction of awesome acceleration.

Much more susceptible were the singles and pairs, the barracuda that would find those unexplainable circles of white sand that glow like sequins among dark tangles of turtle grass. In the heart of those circles, I learned from my uncountable drifts, often a barracuda lay, a dark, emerald hyphen motionless in the sandy center.

Now, if you cast beyond the circle's outer rim and then strip quickly so the fly darts as frantically as a panicked needlefish, and you pull that fly just past that barracuda's long and toothy nose, then, if it is ready to play the game, the log will twitch, turn as it becomes a living predator, and then begin swimming after your fly, keeping its nose an inch or two behind. When it seems as if the fly must bump the hull, sweep the rod so the lure spurts ahead one last time.

Properly provoked, the barracuda will eat the fly just when you think it won't. It will grab it at boatside, turn and rocket away, leaping as it goes, turn back charging toward you, leaping again, turning again, and in general comporting with all the adrenaline and stamina and acrobatics of any game fish you can name.

When at last it wearies and arrives alongside, its silver flanks brilliant under the sun, be cautious, for its teeth never tire. All my flies are barbless, so it is almost always an easy release. If the hook is stubborn, I pry it free with long-handled pincers built like a surgeon's hemostat.

I have never killed a barracuda. I love them too much. For it was they in their wonderful fecundity and ubiquitous presence that gave my solo days their meaning.

However barren those thin waters might have looked, barracuda were always there—there, I would tell myself, for me. There to keep a dream alive. There to make precarious finances and problematic boats worth every anxious spasm.

In the course of my watery wanderings across eight years, I found places where particular barracudas were almost always in residence. It was their turf, but we recognized each other and they would nod at my casts and sometimes they would chase the fly, water hissing, right to the boat, where each of us would look at the other, making contact, the black barracuda eye peering upwards from its brilliantly colored head, looking me over, probing my soul.

Then the fish would be gone, both of us knowing we would likely meet again.

One languorous, late June afternoon when the water stretched leaden under the heat of a windless day, I drifted a narrow byway off Jack Channel, hunting tarpon laid up, dozing until the cooler dark.

Ahead, perhaps fifty feet off the bow, a great shape materialized, a stocky, six-foot torpedo with a back almost as broad as mine. It was there, dark in the green water, a foot below the surface, a mighty presence I assumed to be a tarpon or a shark, perhaps a bull shark.

But as I drifted closer, the silhouette shape of the pointed nose told me it had to be a barracuda, the largest I would ever see. So huge it still visits my dreams.

I cast the tarpon fly, let it sink until it reached the giant's depth. Then I moved it across his nose, past it, and back to the boat. Again, once more.

That great barracuda never twitched. At last my boat was above him. I could see the black orb of his stone-still eye. It stared at me.

Then the big fish sank, settled without motion into the channel's deep until I could see it no more.

But of course, I see it still.

TARPON TIME

Brad Burns

UST AFTER DAYBREAK WE EASED THE SKIFF ONTO A FLAT ON THE OCEAN side of a tiny finger of land just across from Key West Harbor. As Jeffrey instructed, I stood ready with the 12-weight line stripped onto the deck while he poled us in with the light sea breeze against a falling tide. It is the style of guides of Jeffrey's caliber to constantly chatter: keeping the angler informed, building his confidence, helping him to prepare for his first shot at a tarpon.

Almost by us when it first appeared, a pod of tarpon rolled and gulped on the surface. The water was still dark, the surface ruffled by the dawn breeze. The tarpon flashed copper with huge black eyes in the first gleam of daylight.

Jeffrey's calm demeanor disappeared and he leapt around the poling platform like an acrobat in his frantic efforts to turn us around for a shot at the fish. They were gone in an instant. Suddenly the breeze seemed cool, even to someone just one day out of Maine. Is this the way it will be? I was truly fearful that hooking a tarpon might be more than I had bargained for.

Jeffrey climbed from the poling platform, smiled, and said, "It's a great morning. I feel the Marquesas calling us." We ran down the ocean side out around Woman Key and headed west for a thin, green line on the horizon. Back in Maine, I had been told about the Marquesas. Turtle grass flats with winding narrow channels surrounded by a ring of mangrove islands. Tropical birds, wildly leaping needlefish, giant turtles, myriads of snappers, jacks and fish of all kinds, including the hoped-for tarpon; these, I was told, were the fruits of a trip to the Marquesas.

LAUGHING GULL

Larus atricilla

When the tarpon are rolling in the warm days of late spring and summer, the laughing gull's head is a fine jet black. This small coastal gull flits just above the surface, picking tiny fish from the sea as daintily as a humming-bird sips nectar.

My musings were ended when Jeffrey told me that the angler aboard the skiff a few hundred yards ahead of us had just hooked up. I remember clearly the huge silver shape that launched itself at the end of that angler's fly line. The tarpon seemed like a movie creation, too large for the setting. Shining in the sun and throwing off water in all directions, the monster fell back on its side and was gone. "He lost him," Jeffrey said. He knew every move of the angler instinctively and saw the change in posture before the angler's limp arms at his side told me of his loss. Minutes later we could see strings, daisy chains, and moving pods of tarpon all along the now sun-drenched flats on the west side of the Marquesas. Tarpon straightened hooks, ran off hundreds of yards of line, threw hooks, landed on and broke Jeffrey's carefully tied leaders until somewhere around number seven or eight I wrestled one of about eighty pounds to the boat.

My first taste turned out to be a feast beyond any reasonable expectations. Carefully casting a tiny cockroach fly in front of a large tarpon and then hitching oneself to the wild ride that ensues is one of fly fishing's greatest thrills.

Set this in the shimmering tropical surroundings of the southern Florida Keys and it becomes a tough act to follow. But I have that perfect act. In the spring, tarpon fishing is a prelude to days of striper fishing on Maine's rugged coast, then a trip further north to Labrador's boreal forests and unspoiled lakes for mammoth brook trout gone from everywhere else on earth, then on to Martha's Vineyard's autumn beaches for albacore and bonito before winter's curtain limits my fishing to fly tying while in my mind I replay memories from all these great places.

With luck, I'll never have to pick a favorite. In the spring, though, when tarpon migrate through the cuts and passes of the Florida Keys, I know where the best place is. Though I've spent so little time there, I too can hear the Marquesas calling me.

ONLY IN KEY WEST

Harlan Franklin

Y CUSTOMER WAS ONE OF THOSE NICE novices you want so much to catch a fish. You know the type. Eager, enthusiastic, and with no experience or skill. A challenge for any flats guide.

We were fishing early in the morning with a gentle southeast breeze. Perfect conditions for tarpon at one of my secret spots. Calm, undisturbed tarpon, loafing just off the edge of the flats in ten feet of water, waiting to slam into any lure cast near them. Ideal fish for a beginner.

Approaching this spot from a distance, I could make out a sailboat in the area we were to fish. As I got closer, I could see it was a catamaran, and it was sitting right on top of where the tarpon like to lie. I was not happy with the circumstances, but since the boat was just sitting there with no signs of life, I hoped the fish wouldn't be spooked.

I cut the engine and put down the electric motor to approach the boat and, I hoped, the fish. Sure enough, several tarpon came up and rolled right by the sailboat. One cast and *boom,* we were hooked up to a hundred-pounder. In Florida, any fish not landed is at least a hundred-pounder. The fish immediately came out of the water with a spectacular leap, landing right next to the catamaran. Two nude torsos popped up from where they had been sleeping on deck, one male, and one very obviously female, looking to see what all the commotion was about.

I've been involved in many a fight with hooked tarpon, but this was just a bit out of the ordinary. The fish liked the catamaran and kept circling it, with us in hot

"GUIDE'S DAY OFF" *Peter Corbin*

pursuit. The couple aboard watched our activities with interest, carrying on a lively conversation with us as we battled the big fish. The guy put a pair of shorts on. The woman remained au naturel the entire time. I think she enjoyed the audience. She was very well endowed, and the audience certainly did enjoy the view.

Unfortunately, after fifteen minutes, five jumps, and six trips around the catamaran, the fish managed to rub the line on the sailboat's bottom and broke off. The battle had spooked the remainder of the school, so we left, somewhat reluctantly.

Key West is certainly a fascinating place to fish. Not only do we have wonderful fishing, but where else in the world could you fight a big tarpon and carry on a conversation with a naked woman at the same time? Only in Key West.

The Slam tournament at Key West is one of three celebrity tournaments held every year to raise money for the fight against cystic fibrosis. It's a fun tournament, one the anglers, guides, and celebrities all enjoy.

It is not as competitive as many tournaments. Most of the anglers pay the healthy entrance fee because they get a kick out of fishing and associating with well-known people in the sports, entertainment, and outdoor fields. The guides enjoy this tournament also, but being typical Keys guides, they like to see their name up on the winner's board, as well.

In the 1992 competition, I had high hopes of seeing my name up on the board. My angler was Jay Walton, one of my "regulars." Jay was an excellent caster and had that rare ability to get the bait to the fish with fly, spin, or casting tackle. He also had an exceptional ability to see fish, better than many guides.

As our celebrity we were fortunate to have Mark Sosin of ESPN's *Salt Water Journal* fame. I'd known Mark for twenty years and was well acquainted with his casting and fishing abilities. No one in the tournament had a better pair of fishermen on their boat. I figured all I had to do was find a few fish, and these two would do the rest.

The first day we caught two permit. Not bad, but just barely good enough to keep us in contention. By noon of the second day we landed, photographed, and released two more permit. We were in the running, but I felt four average-size permit would not top any of the divisions. We desperately needed another fish. Not just a fish, but a big fish.

Considering the afternoon tide, there was one place where I knew big permit were a definite possibility, so we headed for my big-fish spot.

After ten minutes of poling and seeing nothing, I noticed a dark spot two hundred feet away at twelve o'clock. This was an area I knew well, and for certain there wasn't anything to darken the bottom here. It had to be fish. I alerted my anglers. We all stared at the dark area as I poled closer. At two hundred feet the area separated into five very large permit, all three feet in length. Any one of those fish would more than likely be the largest permit caught in the tournament, and put us in serious contention to win at least one division.

I poled the little Hewes slowly and quietly to within seventy feet of the fish. Jay had first shot and cast his crab at the permit. The crab went fifty feet up in the air and landed fifty feet to the right of the fish. As Jay reeled in, Mark made his cast. Again, the crab sailed fifty feet high and fifty feet to the right. The permit was still there and still calm. Jay made his second cast. This time the cast was straight toward the fish, but low and flat, smacking the water twenty feet in front of the boat. Amazingly, the permit still didn't spook. Mark made his second cast. It was exactly like Jay's—low, flat, and smacking the water well short of the fish. The permit tired of the proceedings and swam away. Mark turned to Jay. "You have infected my casting," he said.

What really happened was that the sight of these big fish gave both experts a humbling case of the "jelly knees," also known as "buck fever." I know all about the jelly knees, having had a case or two of it myself, and as a guide I witness this malady on a regular basis. For sure, in this case we had entirely too much time between first seeing the fish and then casting to them. Too much time to think. There is a solution to jelly knees, but it takes just the right set of circumstances.

Several years ago I got a call from Bob McNally, a well-known outdoor writer living in northeastern Florida. Bob's friend Ray wanted to catch a permit in the worst way, and Bob wanted me to see that Ray got his wish. He told me Ray did some guiding up there and was a super angler. It all sounded great to me, so we picked out some good tides and set a date.

Our day was perfect weatherwise: a gentle breeze, good visibility, clear water, and good tides. Best of all the fish were everywhere, and calm enough so we had no trouble poling to within easy casting range. With all this going for us, Ray was having a devil of a time casting the crab to the fish. Ray handled the tackle perfectly, and his casts were straight toward the fish. The problem was, he would stop the cast well short of the fish. To make things worse, he understood exactly what he was doing wrong. Even so, when another permit would show up, he'd do the same thing all over again. A classic example of the jelly knees.

Late in the afternoon, I spotted a permit feeding calmly and happily along the flat. I poled toward the fish to get Ray within casting range. The fish was moving slowly, but away from us, so it was taking me a few minutes to catch up. I could see Ray tensing and realized that the more time he had to think about his cast, the worse the cast would be.

Suddenly, out of nowhere, fifty feet to our left, two permit tails popped up. Ray did what any good fisherman would do. Instinctively, without thinking about it, he cast his crab to the fish, a perfect cast. The crab landed about two feet in front of the fish, and the fish swam to it. Putting its head down and its tail up, it inhaled the crab, just like a good permit was supposed to. Ray set the hook, and like the excellent

GIL DRAKE

angler he was, did a great job of bringing the twenty-pound fish to the boat in only fifteen minutes.

We were lucky having that situation presented to us. Catching that fish completely cured Ray's casting handicap. From then on every cast was right on the money. His severe case of the jelly knees was cured.

Fly fishing in the waters around Key West is outstanding. Bonefish, tarpon, barracuda, and shark will all take a properly presented fly most of the time. Permit will occasionally take a well-presented fly.

We are now inundated with a new generation of fly fishermen we call "yuppie fly fishermen." The guide answers his phone, and after the usual introduction the new prospective customer describes the wonderful fly-casting school he recently attended. Then he launches into a lengthy dissertation on all the trout and salmon he's caught in the three months since learning to fly-cast.

Now we get down to the nitty-gritty. Our hero has read about what a great fly-rod fish the permit is, and he is coming down to catch one. The poor guide has been biting his tongue since he heard the words "trout" and "salmon," which may be great fly-rod fish, but permit, they ain't. If the guide accepts the charter, it's going to be an extremely frustrating trip for him, for the chances of this guy catching a permit are very, very slim. Even with the new flies and improved techniques, it's not easy for even the best fly fishermen to catch permit on any given day. Or week. There are some pretty fair casters with hundreds of tarpon and bonefish under their belts who are still permit virgins.

In defense of our fledgling fly caster, the only way he's going to learn what the flats are all about is to get out there with an experienced guide, one who's been around long enough to develop lots of patience. Patience is a learned trait absorbed by most flats guides. And, if the angler does improve enough to catch a fish or two, the guide has a good customer for years.

The best thing the guide can do with a beginner "yuppie" is simply take him fishing. Forget permit. Forget concentrating on any one species. Take what's there. Catch a lemon shark and a barracuda on a fly. Throw a fly at everything that swims. Use a spinning rod and crab to catch that first permit. Learn to be a fisherman. Walk before you run.

I'll call these two fellows Joe and Bill. Joe called to arrange two days of fishing with me. It was obvious from the conversation that he knew his way around the flats and was a fly fisherman with extensive experience. Joe indicated that Bill was long on enthusiasm and short on ability but eager to learn what it was all about.

Our first day started off with a bang. We saw fish from the beginning. Joe turned out to be a very good caster, and by ten o'clock he had taken his first permit on a fly.

Bill was chomping at the bit. He just couldn't wait to catch his permit, and there were still a good number of fish on the flat. Bill had half a dozen good opportunities, but to be truthful, he couldn't get the fly close to the fish. The conditions were perfect: clear water, bright sun, and a beautiful flat with just the right amount of water on it. A nice ten-knot breeze from behind us and a bit from the left made for ideal casting conditions. A right-handed caster couldn't ask for better.

After the second muffed shot, Bill started complaining about the wind. I told him he was lucky with the speed and direction, and if we had less wind, the fish would be spooky and we wouldn't be able to get near them. I don't think he believed me.

Things got worse in the afternoon. The wind picked up, and I was no longer able to keep the wind at the best angle for casting and still maintain visibility. Not to mention that the fish had become scarce. I could tell Bill was becoming irritated at the circumstances, and Joe wasn't happy either. After all, he would have liked to have fished more, and it had become apparent to us both that Bill wasn't going to catch anything regardless of how long he was on the bow.

The next morning Joe showed up at the dock alone. "I don't know if Bill is coming or not," he said. "At breakfast I explained to him how discouraging and frustrating it is for the guide—working his fanny off poling the boat and looking for fish, knowing there isn't a snowball in hell's chance of his angler catching any fish he found."

Bill did show up, somewhat subdued. I don't recall what we did that second day, but I would if we had caught another permit.

The little lecture Joe gave Bill was certainly true. To begin with, it's much better for a beginning angler to fish alone. That way his lack of ability doesn't discourage his better partner. And he can get more practice. Most importantly, he can learn something about fishing. Without an experienced angler watching, he doesn't have to concentrate on the glamour species. He can cast to everything. By insisting on fishing for permit only, and hogging the bow in his efforts, Bill changed what had begun to be a wonderful fishing experience into a drag for everyone.

I admit to a slight prejudice about some fly fishermen. On the other hand, I delight in taking out a decent fly fisherman. It seems to me that many fly fishermen don't know the joy of making a good presentation, then hooking and landing a great game fish.

I strongly believe that if the novices could lower themselves to pick up a spinning rod, learn to use it, and catch a few fish, then they would become much better fly fishermen. A real fisherman can handle fly, spinning, and casting tackle, and catch fish with all three.

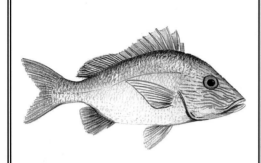

WHITE GRUNT
Haemulon plumieri

When you cannot find another fish, the grunts will be there for you. Likely to be the first fish a child catches off a dock or skiff, grunts are definitely not a threatened species, for they are everywhere a skiff can go off the Lower Keys. A fine panfish, grunts and grits were a Depression staple on Keys dinner plates.

We flats guides are a peculiar lot. We tend to ignore one another out on the flats. Unless, of course, one gets a bit close to another. Then there are apt to be some pleasantries exchanged.

On land, it's a different matter. The guides talk about the fishing, new and old tackle, and their customers, and just generally gossip among themselves, and sometimes, they even play little tricks on one another.

Ten years ago, when I began guiding, I remember hearing about a peculiar bonefishing guide by the name of Mickey. Seems he would not fish Jews, blacks, lawyers, or fly fishermen. Now I'm certain the rumor originated from his friend Bob, who was a natural-born troublemaker.

Now Mickey and I are good buddies, and I found out that this rumor was only half true. Mickey is married to a perfectly charming Jewish lady, and his best customer, who fishes with him several times a year and who has become one of his best friends, is a black IBM executive. However, the part about not fishing lawyers and fly fishermen is true. It works out well for me. When he gets a call from someone wanting to fly fish, he turns the customer over to me. I don't know what he does with the lawyers.

Mickey and Bob used to both fish out of Boog Powell's marina (now Murray's Marina) and were constantly ragging each other. One instance was the time Mickey was sitting in his skiff with two ladies he was fixing to take bonefishing. Bob walked up, looked at the boat and the occupants for a long moment, then exclaimed, "Mickey, you know damn well the judge said you were not allowed to take females out to the backcountry anymore!" He walked off, leaving three somewhat stunned people behind, one with some explaining to do.

Late one afternoon a few days thereafter Bob was away from his boat but his customer was sitting in the boat showing off his twenty-five-pound permit to anyone who would look at it. Remember, a few years ago it was not considered bad form to keep a prize fish, and many were brought in to the dock for mounting, weighing, and photographing.

Mickey walked up and politely listened to a full description of the battle with the fish. Then he commented, "That sure is a big fish. You must own some mighty fine tackle." The customer answered that he hadn't brought any tackle with him, and was using Bob's tackle. Mickey answered, "You mean you landed that permit on Bob's tackle? Mister, you have got to be one of the world's best anglers!" He walked off, leaving behind a speechless and confused fisherman.

Back in those days, Bob fished a lot with his friend Gil. Gil had just bought a new skiff, and the two headed out to look for bonefish in the new boat. They fooled around for a while on the front side, and didn't find anything, so decided to cross through to the backcountry on the Gulf side. Gil headed toward Boca Chica Bay to cut over to the Gulf.

Bob stopped him. "Let's cut through by Shark Key," he said. "It's a lot closer."

Ever-cautious Gil replied, "I've never been that way. Let's go the way we know."

Bob assured Gil that he was completely familiar with the Shark Key route and said there was plenty of water if you knew where to go. Off they went in Gil's new boat and new motor, through Shark Channel, across the bay to the bridge, then past the bridge to Shark Key.

Bang, bang, crunch, and *crunch* again!

The water around Shark Key is very shallow and very hard. They were lucky. The prop was badly damaged, but the lower unit remained intact, and they only had a few minor scratches on the hull. Gil was able to limp back to the marina. Now Gil knows every foot of the shallows around Key West, but he still doesn't like the

Shark Key route to the backcountry. And if he's out with Bob he ignores any route suggestions.

There is no place like Key West for fish and fishermen. The great advantage of being a flats guide here is the people you have for customers. Those who fish the flats, with very, very few exceptions, are gentlemen and sportsmen, people who love the beauty and life that are in the vast area of shallow water surrounding our little island.

CORMORANT VS. BULL SHARK

Dave Harris

N A WINDY MARCH MORNING, MY BROTHER KEN AND I were aboard his twenty-seven-foot fishing boat coming back from a thirty-mile rendezvous with a shrimp trawler. Both of us are light tackle guides working out of Key West, where Ken has been guiding for more than sixteen years; I'm beginning my sixth. With our chum on board we started back to Key West harbor to fish for tarpon.

As we neared the Marquesas, Ken said, "Why don't we catch a cuda and fish for sharks on the flats around the Marquesas? The tarpon won't be biting until the tide changes."

It was a typical day west of Key West. Choppy, clear water. Royal blue skies. Plenty of birds overhead and baitfish being busted along the edges of the flats. A flats skiff is the traditional method, but it is common practice among the Key West light tackle guides to use their larger center-console boats to fish shallow water. Of course, the boat must be equipped with an outboard, or inboard-outboard, that can be tilted high enough to clear the bottom of the boat.

When we're after barracuda, we prefer to use Sea Bees with the first set of treble hooks removed. A floating lure that resembles a ballyhoo, the Sea Bee comes with a plastic lip that makes it swim underwater, but by breaking off the lip and retrieving the lure quickly, you can make it appear to be a small ballyhoo skipping across the surface, fleeing for its life.

I cast to a likely area and began my retrieve. Almost immediately a fifteen-pound cuda came streaking after my lure. I started reeling as fast as I could, making my lure flee for its life. The three-and-a-half-foot cuda was greyhounding across the surface, mouth open, intent on its prey. I heard Ken shout, "Will you let him catch it!"

I slowed down and the cuda nabbed the lure. I set the hook and took delight in the aerial acrobatics of a vastly underestimated game fish.

Too many times I have heard an angler say, "Aw, it's only a cuda." I understand being disappointed in not hooking the fish you are searching for, but a cuda can be an extremely exciting fish. I know of no hooked fish that jumps as high or as quickly, and I have frequently seen cudas leap over my boat when hooked. Fifteen feet in the air is child's play. There are reports of hooked barracuda jumping into boats and biting the offending angler, or anyone else in the way. But where a cuda lands is not intentional; they'll bite anything that gets too close to their mouth. It's all one dangerous accident.

I landed my barracuda, and it quickly became shark bait. Ken cut a fillet partially down the side of the fish, leaving it still attached. Using a large metal clip on a rope, Ken hung the fish over the side, with its head slightly out of the water. We maneuvered the boat to the edge of a good long flat. Raising the engine, we allowed the wind to push us onto and along the flat. Barracuda are oily and strong smelling. In no time we had a good scent slick and we waited.

With Ken watching for the first shark to appear, I decided to examine the cooler full of chum. There were probably 150 pounds of dead fish, crabs, shrimp, and other bottom dwellers. I started throwing away the sponges, starfish, and shells. Anything I found alive went overboard.

"There's a cormorant behind the boat. Throw back a couple of the smaller snapper and grunts for him." Ken said.

I looked up. A nearly black cormorant with bright, emerald-green eyes was floating on the surface about twenty feet from the boat. He was checking out the trash I was dumping overboard. I threw a couple of small fish to him, and they were grabbed, played with and swallowed the minute they hit the water. Cormorant are excellent underwater swimmers. They use only their large, webbed feet for propulsion, and occasionally their wings for quick turns. They have no oil on their feathers, which allows them to swim extremely fast after their favorite food—small fish. I had thrown almost half a dozen fish before Ken alerted me. "Here comes our first shark. Looks like a bull shark. Could weigh around two hundred pounds," he said.

While reaching for a rod I recalled how often my customers had asked me what would happen if a shark and a cormorant met underwater. It looked as though I was about to find out. I felt a sympathetic pang of regret. Bull sharks have a reputation for being aggressive. The shark was hot on the barracuda slick. You could tell he was intent on finding something to eat, preferably a dead cuda. The cormorant was still swimming back and forth near the stern of the boat, looking for any scraps that might be available.

Two hundred pounds of shark spotted five pounds of bird and glided over to investigate. The bird wasn't aware of the shark until it was five to six feet away. As soon as the cormorant spotted the shark he did the one thing that most people would not have expected. He charged. Like a little torpedo he shot through the water directly at the head of the shark, which immediately turned tail and ran. The cormorant turned back to the boat. Thinking that he had definitely earned it, I threw him a small lane snapper.

Then I heard, "Dave, that shark is gonna get that bird. Here he comes!"

The bull shark had darted off, made a large circle, and was coming straight back for the cormorant. This time the bird wasn't aware of its approach. Ken and I stood silently, watching one of nature's life-and-death struggles.

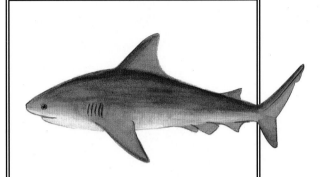

BULL SHARK
Carcharhinus leucas

A frequent visitor to the flats, the bull shark is a heavyset aggressor with a rounded snout and a brutal approach to hooked or injured fish. The heavyweight flats predator, bulls reach ten feet in length and are a potential danger to waders, especially in murky or blooded waters.

The cormorant was floating on the surface, his back to the approaching shark. His head was underwater searching the bottom for anything he might have missed.

Intent only on the cormorant, the shark came in with no hesitation. When he was only five feet away, he started to roll onto his side so his jaws could reach the bird on the surface. Ken and I both expected to see bird feathers floating when this was over. Suddenly, when the shark was almost upon him, the cormorant whirled and nailed the shark on the tip of his snout. The big fish nearly flip-turned, slamming his tail on the surface, water flying in all directions. The shark headed quickly for deeper water and we never saw it again. As for the cormorant, with no further delay, he leapt out of the water and landed on our stern, wings spread to dry.

Super Bird had prevailed. Woe to any shark that thought this was an easy meal.

We were impressed. Five-pound bird, two-hundred-pound shark. Tough bird!

I have been bitten by a cormorant while trying to remove a hook from its beak. I can honestly say that they bite hard. The beak is hooked, and they twist tenaciously before releasing. No comparison to a shark bite, but not bad for a five-pound bird. That cormorant reinforced what I have told so many people who asked me what to do when confronted with a shark. Aggressive behavior, I tell them, will usually chase a shark away. That little bird definitely made a believer out of me.

DAVID HARRISON WRIGHT

CAPTAIN BILLY
from KILLING ME SOFTLY

John Leslie

HE ANNUAL BENEFIT DANCE PORTIA VILLANI HAD ASKED ME to play was less than a week away, on Thursday. Saturday morning I called around to make sure that arrangements had been made for the piano and amplifying equipment I would need. Then I called Judge Watson.

On weekends I knew that Just, an enthusiastic fisherman, liked to spend time on the water. This morning, however, a squall line was hanging off the southeastern horizon and we'd been getting intermittent rain accompanied by strong gusts of wind all morning. The weather forecast included a small-craft advisory, so I called to see if the judge would like to go to lunch.

"Can't make it today," Just said. "Weather permitting, I'm taking the boat out tomorrow, though, if you want to go fishing."

It had been years since I'd been on a fishing boat. Captain Billy used to take me out once in a while on the *Low Blow,* and I would help the mate bait and set the outriggers while clients sat in the deck chairs, drinking beer and waiting for something to strike their own baited hooks. We trolled along the edge of the Gulf Stream, the boat wallowing in the dark blue waters, as our eyes scanned astern for a sailfish or a marlin to break the surface and jump our lines. I found it monotonous and, on the times when those big fish did take the bait and the mate set the hook and handed the rod to a beery-eyed client who fought the fish for a couple of hours, sad. My stomach was always queasy, and the sight of one of those monstrous fish lying dead on the deck of the boat, bleeding, the color draining from its body, left me filled with a kind of nameless dread.

I never said anything to Captain Billy, who would only have laughed. He never seemed quite so happy as on days when he caught fish and had his picture taken with his client, standing on the dock next to a fish that hung from a block and tackle, its weight chalked on its ghastly side.

The morning I was called at the police station to come to the boat where I found my father lying on his stomach in the wheelhouse, his head in a puddle of blood, I felt that same sense of dread. It was as if there were some tragic fate awaiting those of us who had participated in the mindless slaughter of these creatures, beginning with my father; some retribution that would be claimed for our arrogance.

From the day I carried Captain Billy's body from the *Low Blow,* I never again set foot on another deep-sea sport-fishing boat. A few times I had been on powerboats zooming around the harbor, less often on sailboats, but the sea held too much mystery for me, and despite my heritage, I acknowledged my anxiety.

Judge Watson was primarily a fly fisherman who seemed to fish more for the solace of being alone on the water than for anything he might catch, which, in any case, he released once he'd brought it to the boat.

We left at dawn Sunday morning, flying west to the Marquesas over the shallow water of the flats in the judge's ancient twenty-foot skiff with a 150-HP Evinrude hanging off the stern. It had been years since I'd last been here, but it was a primeval scene, unchanged over time except for the debris that reflected our age: Styrofoam cups, plastic wrappers, and aluminum cans washed up into the mangroves and deserted dune beaches.

Just maneuvered the skiff back into one of the many lagoons inside the Marquesas, surrounded by mangroves, and cut the engine. The water back here was placid as a lake, an ice sky flushed by the rising sun. Diamondlike projectiles of light shot off the water in the distance where wading birds stood motionless as death, their long-

GREAT EGRET
Casmerodius albus

Almost as large as the great white heron, the great egret is plumed during its breeding season. Once favored by milliners, those pale plumes nearly cost the bird its survival. This stately, long-legged white heron has black legs and feet, a sharp, yellow bill, and leans forward when it fishes.

necked, grayish bodies frozen against the backdrop of mangroves. Except for the whisper of wavelets lapping around the chine of the boat, there was absolute silence.

For a moment neither of us moved, taking in the scene, the sudden cessation of sound and activity, before Just set fire to a cigar, then lifted a couple of spinning rods from their rack, handing one to me. It was fitted with a green plastic tube lure, around stainless-steel leader wire that tied onto the line. The tip of a hook glinted through one end of the lure. I recognized a cuda rig as I watched Just move up into the bow and begin blindcasting for the powerful, missile-shaped barracuda.

After yesterday's blow the water here, though calm, was still murky, limiting our ability to see the fish, which was why Just was using a spinning rod rather than a fly rod. I stood at the stern and made a few blind casts myself into the mirrored water, but after a few minutes I was content to sit down and watch Just, his back to me, as he cast and retrieved line, a cloud of cigar smoke occasionally billowing over his head.

This kind of fishing had been too still, too tame for Captain Billy. He needed to hear the thump of the engines, be at the wheel to feel the momentum, shouting instructions over the drone of the engines, exercising some measure of control over his sea world. This silent drifting was too haphazard for a man like my father, a man used to imposing himself on nature. The difference between Captain Billy and Just Watson was the difference between night and day, I thought.

Nearly half an hour passed while Just continued casting, without a word and without catching a fish. When he finally came back to the cockpit, the judge grinned. "Bud, I thought you were a fisherman."

"It's been a few years. I was just thinking about Captain Billy, the days on the *Low Blow.*"

"Not quite the same thing."

"A far cry."

"Let's take a look over here. I've caught permit a few times in the past on the south side." Just started the motor and we eased over just above an idle to the other end of the lagoon. Other than a cormorant or two taking off from the water, their black tail feathers dripping water, the wading birds weren't disturbed.

Skittish permit inhabited these shallow waters and fed by nosing into the bottom muck in search of crabs. As they did, their tails sometimes broke the surface, marking their location for a sharp-eyed fisherman.

When we were drifting once more, the motor off, Just picked a live crab from the bottom of a bait bucket and put it on a hook on another spinning rod, then went forward and, dangling the crab over the side, scanned the water. I saw nothing. The tails were dark, like triangular flags, and exceptionally difficult to see against the water.

Moments later, I was amazed when Just flipped back his rod and cast. "See him?" he asked quietly.

"No." I saw the crab land about twenty yards to the front and left of the boat, and as Just began reeling in, there was a sudden splash of water when Just struck the fish. Line began to zing off his reel. Permit were savage fighters, and for the next twenty minutes the two played one another until Just finally brought him alongside the boat, picked him up, and took the hook from his mouth. Then, cradling the fish in both hands, Just gently moved the permit back and forth along the surface of the water, pumping air into its gills. When he was released, the permit darted away.

Sweating, Just came back, got a thermos of coffee, and sat down behind the wheel. "All there is to it," he said.

"Sure. Care to repeat it?"

"Shit. A man gets one or two of those a year, he's lucky. Like looking for a needle in a haystack."

Notes of a Backcountry Bumbler

John Graves

I WAS WELL INTO MY SIXTIES WHEN I FIRST VISITED THE FLORIDA KEYS, lured by my brother-in-law, John Cole, a transplanted Downeaster who was living there and later became the founder and proprietor of the Key West Anglers Club. At the time (let us shun from the start any pretense of expertise), I had only recently begun to use my fly rods in salt water. In the years that followed that first trip, however, though still attached to hinterland roots fifteen hundred miles distant from the paradise of the vanished Calusa, I kept trying in a somewhat poky and geriatric way to make up for lost time, traveling down there at least a couple of times each year for stays of up to a month, and spending as much time on the water as daylight, weather, and stamina allowed.

By far the best of the fishing was on chartered expeditions out of Key West with guides like Jeffrey Cardenas and Michael Pollack. But personal economics, combined with a penchant for doing things the hard way, led also to a great deal of bumbling about on my own. Sometimes I went out by myself, but usually with my wife, Jane, or Brother John Cole or some other friend. These unprofessional outings involved not only fishing but exploring unknown corners, getting lost or stuck from time to time, observing birds and strange water creatures, anchoring in mangrove nooks for lunch, and other feckless activities. Maybe fishing itself is feckless, of course, but that fact doesn't bother me much. My favorite area for such nosing about came to be the stretch of the Gulfside backcountry from the Water Keys and the Contents to Johnston Key, and sometimes west to the Snipes and beyond. It is accessible from any of the launching ramps near U.S. 1 between Big Pine and Cudjoe, or even from Key West if you've got a fast boat and a fair-sized gas tank. Much of the time, especially on weekdays, you can have a piece of it to yourself. Blue-water craft raise violent wakes along the main channels as they head to or from the Gulf, but the flats in general, with their narrow, tortuous channels and their mangrove keys and islets, are not heavily disturbed by people.

There are reasons for this shortage of humanity. For one thing, much of the backcountry is a complex maze and not easy for outlanders to navigate, especially now that the authorities have yanked out the old numbered inland waterway markers that showed on charts—yanked them out as part of a program of cleanup and preservation, which of course is praiseworthy, if a bit hard on bumblers. Other landmarks exist that can help a little, though some of them may also be slated for removal in that same campaign—noticeable items like the abandoned white geodesic dome on Sawyer, the Coast Guard observation blimps at the northern tip of Cudjoe, the Australian pines on Tarpon Belly Key, and the ragged mangroves of Raccoon, plucked half-bare by bored rhesus monkeys that live there and are destined for interesting experiences in laboratories. But such known spots don't usually mean a lot when you're trying to get from one place to another across intricate waters.

In clear, relatively calm weather the water can be read—pale blue over sand, dark blue in the channels, dark green over deeper turtle grass flats, brown or whitish over shallow expanses of sand or mud or coral, and so on. But a confirmed bumbler can have visited a specific area time and again under good conditions, and can think he's got it memorized, and then there will be a clouded, windy day when shallows and deeps are all the same dull, ruffled shade of gray. On such a day he will quite likely find himself up to his knees in marly muck three or four or more times, labor-

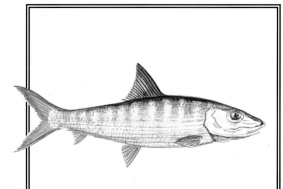

BONEFISH
Albula vulpes

Small cousin of the tarpon, the bonefish, pound for pound, is an equal or better fighter. Elusive by nature, the bonefish's pale colors and wary approach make it difficult to see. And once seen, it is likely to spook at anything but a precise and delicate presentation. "There goes a bonefish," is a line heard frequently on Lower Keys waters.

YELLOW STINGRAY

Urulophus jamaicensis

The smallest of the painful stingrays (each has a toxic stinger near the base of its tail), the yellow stingray is your least likely accident on the flats off the Keys. Like the southern stingray, these rays also hide under a layer of sand, but they are neither as large nor as numerous.

ing profanely in an effort to wallow his boat back to floatable water. If he's truly lucky he'll whack a coral head or a hard bottom with his outboard's costly lower unit, after which he will be magically cured of ambitions to cowboy all over the place with aplomb, like the guides and locals he has envied.

Nor is the fishing in that stretch of backcountry usually as great as it can be elsewhere in the lower Keys. Though it holds tarpon in season, there are not many of the kind of medium-depth flats on which beyond Key West and the Northwest Channel those noble fish visibly cruise and roll and daisy-chain, prime targets for one's flies. You can stake off on the windward side of a channel in the backcountry and wait for fish to show briefly, then start blind-casting to where you think they may have been headed, but that can be a pretty dreary procedure if no fish takes after fifty or a hundred throws with a #12 rod, as nearly always happens. Several years of sporadic efforts of this sort by the varying crew of our skiff (efforts that grew less frequent as disillusionment burgeoned) produced two or three tarpon that jumped once or twice and threw the hook, a number of swirls and follows, and one fish of eighty pounds or so that was brought almost to the boat by my daughter Sally, before the line snapped with a twang at the nail knot. (Yes, I know that knot is supposed to be retied from time to time, but I hadn't done it that year. . . .)

Even when tarpon are behaving classically in a classic place, for that matter, I have learned in my usual hard way that they aren't really an appropriate objective for amateurs, at any rate aging ones. For instance, I pole reasonably well, at least when there's not much wind, but I can't pole and fish at the same time without a lot of clatter, and as a pole-lady my Jane, bless her, tends to move the boat in tight concentric circles. Our combined ineptitudes reached a fitting climax one day at gray dawn in a spot not far from Sugarloaf, with no wind, no other boats in sight, a strong incoming tide, and pod on pod of large tarpon working happily and noisily in slick water all around us. We tried to sneak up on some of them quietly without success, then staked off and waited for a pod to come within casting range. When one bunch finally did, I managed to bonk the lead fish on the head with a weighted Cockroach, whereupon the whole pod spooked with great sucking and slurping sounds and hauled tail at top speed in the general direction of Cuba.

In slight mitigation, I might note that during those same years, on chartered expeditions with guides, we were hooking and jumping and bringing in our fair share of *Megalops atlanticus* and having a fine time doing it. Muscular, hardworking, osprey-eyed skippers made all the difference, even though they weren't able to prevent us from bumbling entirely. Ask Jeffrey about the time I connected with a sixty-pounder in a fast outgoing tidal "river" near Woman Key and ended up somehow facing aft with the line smoking out forward between my legs. Or ask Michael about the morning when Jane and I hooked four good ones in a row and each time fouled the slack line on something—a fighting butt, a rod rack, some part of a human anatomy—before it cleared the stripping guide. Michael was using twenty-pound class tippets that day, and they broke with great reluctance, making line that was wrapped around something—like my hand, for example—tighten like a garrote when the fish hit the end of things. There are lots of laughs aboard a tarpon boat. . . .

Bonefish are different, ideally suited to the purposes of a lone-wolf amateur, or so the theory goes. Said theory would seem to have been borne out by my first experience with them in those backcountry waters—or anywhere else, to be honest—in my second year in the Keys. During that winter in my barn at home in Texas, inspired by tarpon charters the spring before, I had fitted out a little fiberglass hull in approximation of a flats skiff and had dubbed it Old Fart, though without putting the name on the transom.

In April, equipped with fishing literature, charts, information from friends, and the names of people to look up along the way, I hitched the boat's trailer to my pickup and set out on a meandering lone-wolf journey along the Gulf coast toward Key West, where Jane was to meet me in late May. Spring being tardy that year, the weather stayed wettish, windy, and sharp from the Sabine to the Cedar Keys and below, so the fishing was generally lousy along that whole vast reach of shore. The water was still too cold, and often murky besides.

I did catch some pleasant black bass on hair bugs in the marshes south of Lake Charles, managed to get totally lost for several hours in the dark watery forest of the great Atchafalaya Swamp with alligators roaring their spring love songs all around, got into the big shellcracker bream of the Suwannee and saw a manatee near its mouth, chose a motel in Fort Myers that turned out to be that night's rendezvous for the local drug dealers, and had various other mild adventures. I met some good people too, and fished with a couple of them. But my main objective—vigorous, fly-gobbling saltwater species—stayed elusive until I got to the Ten Thousand Islands and the Everglades, where a handful of redfish and speckled trout and a couple of acrobatic ladyfish somewhat revived my sense of possibility.

The Keys came next. At home before starting out I had conferred over charts with a younger friend named Robert, a far more gifted angler than I have ever been, who a good many years earlier, in his twenties, had spent months fishing the Keys on his own, with plenty of success. Since his flotation at that time had consisted of a car-top canoe, the marks he made on my charts were just about all within paddling range of U.S. 1, but knowing that he knew whereof he spoke, I made notes.

Thus it was that one morning in early May I drove from my motel to a boat ramp near the northern edge of a development on Big Pine Key, where I launched and ran a short distance to a little marl flat splotched with turtle grass and tucked among clumps of mangrove. Nobody else was there, though I could see women sunbathing and hanging out laundry beside houses not too far away.

The tide was low and incoming and nothing seemed to be moving on the flat, so I staked off at its edge and settled down for a wait, sitting on the bow with my feet dangling in the water and my #8 bass rod beside me on the casting deck. Its reel was a freshwater Hardy, already pocked and stained from only a little use in the salt, despite nightly washings. In honor of Friend Robert in that place, the fly I had tied on was an unassertive #6 tan affair with a cocked-up tail that he calls the Baited Breath.

A hundred and fifty yards away, a little flock of white pelicans were weaving about like cutting horses as they herded small school fish into a niche against an islet, and I watched while the quarry tried frantically to break out of the trap and the birds started snatching them up. There is no shortage of mayhem in the water, a fact that I somehow find reassuring, although I can't say just why. Maybe it means that mankind's own habitual violence is just a way of conforming to nature's rhythms.

Events closer at hand, however, abruptly seized my attention. Bonefish had arrived on the flat. Except in pictures I had never seen one to recognize it, but when they showed up they were unmistakable. They were suddenly everywhere in water a foot or so deep—waving their tails in the air, mudding, making humpy wakes, and doing the other things that the books said they ought to do. Most were quite large, at least to my eye at that moment.

Easing down into the water, I stripped line from the reel and hoped that I wouldn't have to wade far on the mushy bottom. I didn't. Quite soon a little pod of three or four good fish came working diagonally toward me, making a mud. When they were in range I laid the fly out ahead of them. It fell a little short of their course, but the lead fish saw it and darted aside to grab it. Thirty minutes or so of lovely powerful runs and lovely screaming from the click-drag reel ensued before I got him

BLACK GROUPER

Mycteroperca bonaci

Any of the groupers is an extremely difficult fly-rod catch. For as soon as they feel the hook, groupers will dart to their nearby coral refuge and dig in. It takes a stout rod and rig to yank them clear. But they have a fine appetite for artificial lures and are stubborn fighters.

Tickled Pink

FL 8180 GN

in, twenty-eight inches long and weighing eight pounds or more, and evidently still quite healthy when I turned him loose after some swishing to and fro.

I climbed back onto the casting deck and sat basking in satisfaction for a time, then started fishing for that one's brothers and sisters that were still on the flat. They liked the Baited Breath. I jerked it out of the mouths of the next three that tried to eat it but hooked a fourth, which made a commotion in a shallow place on his first run toward the channel, spooking the rest to the deeps. On the second run I somehow got a loop of slack line around my little finger and that, of course, was that.

It was a couple of years later before I fully understood what unbelievable luck I had had in taking a respectable bonefish on my first cast ever to that species, and what brought understanding was the realization that in the whole two years I had not caught another, despite a good bit of trying. I had learned too that bonefish are not all that common in the backcountry of the lower Keys, west of the Seven Mile Bridge. We found some from time to time in places like the hard-bottomed flat north of Johnston, the beautiful nestled one at Riding, the grassy ones inside the Water Keys, and the jagged coral shallows at the northwest tip of Raccoon, where the rhesus monkeys watched our endeavors with stolid interest from the shade of tattered mangroves. Usually these bonefish we found were skittish, however, and on the two or three occasions when they weren't, I exhibited great dexterity in snatching the fly away from them as they charged it, or in letting the tippet tick coral when one did happen to hook himself. So much for theory. . . .

In fact, I didn't catch another until I went with Friend Robert to Andros Island, where the bonefish were as numerous as stars, and were avid for Baited Breaths.

Mainly what we went after on our own in the backcountry in recent times were the less glamorous species that reside there, and with them success was less elusive, though by no means spectacular. A measure of its unspectacularity may be the fact

"THREE MEN IN A BOAT" *Peter Corbin*

that I remember most of the fish of any size at all that were caught on those expeditions, and also many that weren't caught. These remembered fish include small sharks taken on popping bugs, especially a doughty blacktip in the Outer Narrows of the Snipes; a number of huge gray snappers that dashed from their lairs in the tangled roots of mangroves to grab a fly, then surged inexorably back into the tangle and broke me off; and a good many fine barracudas, of which the most impressive was an enormous specimen that seized a small snapper Brother John Cole was bringing in on a #5 freshwater trout rod and reel. This fish hooked himself and made a high-speed, wide, semicircular run, during which he leapt clear of the water four times and exhibited his five feet of glistening length.

John was laughing and pumping his elbows up and down and waving the little rod after that monster broke free. A main reason I like to go out with him is that he lives his fishing intensely, waxing euphoric when things go right and cursing the skies when they don't. I recall times in flats skiffs when everybody else on board was helpless with laughter as John raged and blasphemed on the casting deck after some mistake, usually involving slack line and his feet, which had cost him a shot at a tarpon.

"Did you see him?" he said now of the cuda. "Did you see that big son of a bitch jump?"

I remember a lot of other things, too. A palolo worm hatch near the northwest tip of Fleming Key and the assembled tarpon going mad but paying no attention to the flies we offered. The pristine and magical Marquesas with nurse sharks thrashing amorously in the shallows, and a time when the hammerheads wrought huge bloody damage among a great school of tarpon (John Cole wrote about that in a book), and the magnificent red, stormy dawnings in the east, and once when I hooked a good fish Jeffrey said, "You'll make my day if you'll jump him against that sunrise," and I did, or rather the lovely tarpon did. The horse conch that pinned down a queen conch and inserted an obscene orange mass of itself into the queen's shell in preparation for the feast. Brown pelicans diving like rockets, herons motionless in the shallows with frigatebirds above, the purposeful arrow flight from key to key of white-crowned pigeons, and cormorants that could look like rolling tarpon until they raised their heads. ("Despicable shags!" Brother John called those.) Huge rays, and porpoises, always porpoises, and pounding wetly homeward across the restless Boca Grande Channel. . . . Plenty of things to remember.

In effect, that fishing and aquatic poking about are now finished, though Jane and I may fly down there another time or two for tarpon charters. The Key West Anglers Club lost its lease and closed its doors in 1993; John Cole is back in Maine writing more books; and I find that I don't really want to return to the Keys for extended stays without having him there to fish and putter and visit with. He and his Jean were a main part of the place as we knew it, an indispensable part in truth.

Another relevant factor is that I am now seventy-four years old, not any more decrepit than is normal for that stage of life, but not a hell of a lot less, either. On occasion I've found myself wishing that I'd come at the Keys and their waters much younger. But there were many other fine things to do in my earlier days, and I doubt the Keys would have meant as much to me back then as they have in later times. A life is built of swatches of experience good or bad or indifferent that eventually become memories, and this particular swatch was superb—the waters and islands and skies and creatures, the friendships with John and Jean and with Jeffrey and Ginny Cardenas and with Jacques and Coco Vivien and others, the tarponeering with bright and capable guides, and even or maybe especially the long-continued private bumbling on the fringes of the Gulf of Mexico. All of those things make up the vivid and recent memory of a world I am most grateful to have known.

BELTED KINGFISHER

Ceryle alcyon

Unmistakable with its broad, white collar and blue-gray plumage, the belted kingfisher has a rattling call that will sound as you approach a mangrove hummock or motor along a narrow canal. These feathered anglers that hover before they dive are the eternally vigilant sentries of the Keys.

THE FISHING DIDN'T COUNT

Brock Apfel

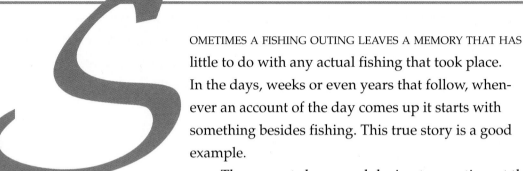OMETIMES A FISHING OUTING LEAVES A MEMORY THAT HAS little to do with any actual fishing that took place. In the days, weeks or even years that follow, whenever an account of the day comes up it starts with something besides fishing. This true story is a good example.

These events happened during tarpon time at the Marquesas in the vicinity of Mooney Harbor and Gull Keys sometime in the late 1970s or early 1980s. The timing is important because it was a time of more fish, no crowds, and (later on you'll see the importance of this) marine sanitation regulations that were more permitting than they are now.

My now departed good friend Sidney and I were fishing with Captain Rick Gardner. Rick and I had fished together for about fifteen years and had developed that easy, friendly and cooperative relationship that transcends that of guide and client. Rick is based in Marathon, and we had trailered down to Garrison Bight and made the run to the Marquesas. We got there about ten in the morning and there was a single other boat, staked out at the southwest corner of the island ring at what we had come to call "Montgomery's Corner."

It was one of those breathless and hot days when the water is glassy flat and the horizon seems to merge indistinguishably with the sky. We staked out on a sandy patch outside the basin in one of the cuts that lead around Mooney Harbor Key into the basin. The occasional lock-jawed tarpon cruised by; our efforts to get them to eat failed with every fly in our arsenal.

After a while we began to hear a commotion from high up on the flat. Whatever was causing it was a long way off, but it was one of those days when a crash-diving pelican a half mile away sounds as if he's next door. We listened and speculated on what was causing the ruckus, and wondered if the noise would attract sharks.

We had about decided to pole onto the flat to see firsthand what was going on. Just as we were getting ready to pick up, a blacktip shark in the seventy- to one-hundred-pound range cruised lazily past about seventy-five yards off the bow. Visibility was perfect, and we could see him as if he were swimming in a fishbowl. I was at the bow and was rigged for tarpon with a 12-weight and a 5/0 Black Death with 15-pound class leader and 12-inch mono shock tippet.

On the off chance that he would hear, I put the rod tip in the water and swished it back and forth. Sure enough, the shark turned and swam directly toward the bow of the boat. As he approached I made a cast my mother would be proud of and let the fly settle until it was three inches directly in front of his left eye. He was now about thirty feet from the boat. It took only one jig of the fly. He rolled his whole body in slow motion, bringing his mouth to the fly and bit. Didn't suck it in, bit it.

All this played out more or less at our feet and in slow motion. I set the hook, which, because of the way he bit it, had the shank across the teeth and the entire leader outside the mouth. The fish took off in a hot blacktip speed run, but never jumped. After an extended tussle, he was brought to the boat, where there was a discussion of just who among us was going to reach down and get the fly back. There being no volunteers, I settled the matter by breaking him off.

The commotion was still resounding on the flat. Deciding in favor of satisfying our curiosity we pushed the boat high to see what was going on. We found a couple of very large nurse sharks, apparently spawning. They were in water too shallow to cover them, and their bright pink bellies glinted in the sun as they thrashed about with water flying everywhere. Just like spawning carp in Missouri.

We took in the scene for a while before deciding to go back to tarpon depth to do

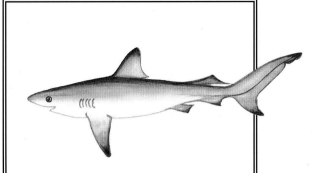

BLACKTIP SHARK

Carcharhinus limbatus

If you see a shark leaping, it's most likely a blacktip. Long-snouted and fast swimming, the blacktip does indeed have fins tipped with black. Growing to about eight feet, blacktips often visit the flats. They will eat a fly and take off on a startling, powerful first run.

what we came for in the first place. While Rick was poling us off the flat, I was seized by the urge to complete nature's morning routine. So, with the ease of men who have spent a lot of time together, I stepped to the transom, lowered my shorts, and assumed the position: feet on the transom, holding on to the poling platform supports. The motor was up and we were in no more than two feet of water. Rick continued to pole from his position on the platform immediately above me while Sidney occupied himself discreetly in the bow. With each push of the pole, the boat rocked gently and I found myself being "dipped" in unison with the motion.

After a few minutes Rick said, in his always calm manner, "If I were you I'd get my cheeks away from the water right now." I thought, yeah, right, another put-on in a string of endless put-ons. I did look at Sidney, though, and his eyes were getting as big as saucers. A quick look down showed why. There, immediately below my rear, was the head of a hammerhead shark wider than any part of me. He had apparently swum right up the chum line to the source. Needless to say, I took Rick's suggestion.

We were back in Marathon by seven.

In the years that have passed I have thought many times about that big nonjumping blacktip on a fly, and the wonder of seeing those huge sharks half out of the water, following nature's plan as they have for eons. Yet to this day, when I talk to Rick about that trip, for some reason my blacktip or the spawning nurse sharks don't seem to get mentioned until very late in the conversation. If at all.

CORBIN'S GRAND SLAM

Peter Corbin

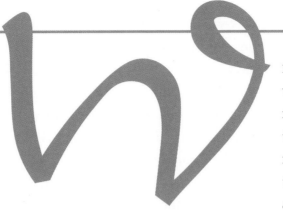

HEN YOUNG MEN FALL IN LOVE, WHETHER with a woman or with a sport, the romance is often fleeting. The test of time proves that what felt like love was really infatuation: intense, yes, but also temporary. Soon, the attraction fades, and attention is focused on a new object of desire.

It is different with older men, men of maturity, experience, and a certain hard-earned wisdom. When they find something they like, they hold and respect it, having learned how easily it can slip away, how suddenly it can be taken.

So it was with my friend John. Relatively late in life, he discovered saltwater fly fishing—flats fishing, to be more precise—and it quickly became his passion. He had much to learn about this difficult, demanding sport, but he possessed the one indispensable quality that made him an ideal student: devotion. He also enjoyed the benefit of a skilled and patient teacher, renowned Florida Keys guide Marshall Cutchin. John took to spending nearly every other day stalking the flats with Marshall. Success proved maddeningly elusive, but when it came, it came in a big, big way. John's first saltwater fish on a fly was a thirty-five-pound permit—a feat comparable to winning the Kentucky Derby, if not the entire Triple Crown, with the first thoroughbred you ever owned. The odds against it were astronomical. Just ask any of the legion of saltwater fly fishermen who have yet to land a permit of any description, and not for want of trying.

Despite the magnitude of his achievement, however, John remained humble. "Even a blind hog occasionally finds an acorn," he shrugged. And instead of slackening, his interest in flats fishing only intensified. It was with great pleasure, then, that I accepted a commission from John's children to paint a portrait of their father at this new sport that so fascinated and fulfilled him.

The necessary arrangements were made, and in late February I gladly left the snow and ice of upstate New York behind and flew to balmy, sun-drenched Key West. At my request, John had booked Marshall's services for three consecutive days. Two days are normally all I need to amass sufficient reference photographs for a commissioned painting; I also use this time to develop a feel for the personality of the subject, and a sense of place. The final painting is a distillation of all these ingredients, which is why—I hope—it succeeds not just on a visual level, but on an emotional level as well. I'd budgeted three days just to be on the safe side in case of bad weather. If the weather held, well, maybe I could sneak out and do a little fishing with Marshall myself. John had already informed me that he'd probably have to spend one of the three days at his office.

Tom Rowland, a top western trout guide who was learning the ins and outs of flats fishing and studying for his saltwater captain's license, volunteered to provide the "camera boat" for me while I took pictures of John and Marshall. Early on, John was self-conscious about being photographed, but gradually he loosened up and settled into an easy casting rhythm. Although the fish were uncooperative, the play of light on the flats was dazzling. I knew that the images being recorded on film were strong, evocative ones that would serve me well back in the studio.

The following day, Tom had other obligations, so I went out with John and Marshall. John was far more relaxed, and I snapped a number of photos of him with a wide-angle lens while he cast to barracuda and permit. I even took a couple of casts at

permit myself. They acted like just about every other permit I'd cast to in my ten-year quest, utterly disdainful. That afternoon, the water smooth as glass and the air drowsy with heat, we both jumped nice tarpon in the sixty- to seventy-pound class. They treated us to several gill-plate-clattering leaps before throwing our hooks, and I was reminded again of how immensely powerful these fish are.

By now, I had more than enough reference material for the painting. With another gorgeous day predicted, I tried to persuade John to put his work on the back burner and go fishing. He wavered, but then decided that he simply had to take care of business. In his absence, I asked Marshall if Tom could come along. Now, asking an established Keys guide to let an "apprentice" tag along is like asking a stockbroker to show his buy list to a trainee. A lot of guides would have told me where to put their push pole—or even offered to help put it there. Marshall, on the other hand, couldn't have been more accommodating. "Sure, that'd be fine," he said. Then, smiling slyly, he added, "We won't show him too much that isn't already common knowledge."

A flimsy scrim of clouds gave way to brilliant sunshine, and the flats became an illuminated stage. At nine-thirty, I was standing on the casting platform while Marshall poled. He and Tom scanned the middle distance for fish. Glen Blackwood, a former national sales director for Scott Power-Ply, had sent me a new 9-foot, 9-weight rod to try, and with permit being the order of the day (we hoped), I tied on a Del's Merkin, a crab pattern created by Del Brown of Key West, the man who has probably caught more permit on a fly than anybody else.

After spending the winter holed up in my studio, I wasn't entirely confident in my ability to spot fish on the shimmering flats. So when something caught my eye virtually within spitting distance of the boat, I turned to Marshall for clarification. "Um, Marshall," I queried, "what's that at three o'clock?"

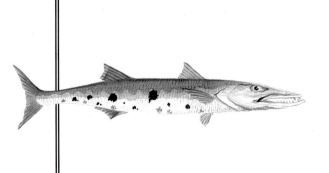

GREAT BARRACUDA

Sphyraena barracuda

Look for dark, jade logs motionless on the pale flats under a January sun. For in the cooler months when water temperatures drop, the barracuda comes in from the sea searching for the warmth of thin waters. How fortunate for the angler, for this magnificent fish readily eats lures and then fights like a champion.

"It's a permit," he replied, as blasé as if he were pointing out a robin on the front lawn. "Let him go past, and I'll swing the boat. Okay—he's at fifty feet, heading right."

"Got him," I said. Or at least I thought I saw him; the fish seemed to materialize and dematerialize at will, like a capricious specter. I cast anyway.

"You're too far in front of him," Marshall advised. "Pick up and cast again."

The second cast was closer to the mark, but the result remained the same. "Try again, right at him," urged Marshall. Certain that I'd line him, I dropped the Merkin inches from the fish's nose. "Perfect," Marshall said, sotto voce. And it was, too, because the permit ate the fly as purposefully and unhesitatingly as if he'd been waiting his whole life to do it. There was a microsecond of terror when a coil of loose line partially wrapped around my arm, but I frantically cleared it, got the fish on the reel, and let him run. It was a new sensation for me; the four permit I'd previously hooked had broken off in a heartbeat. But that was in Belize. In the Keys, with no coral to contend with, I felt I had a fighting chance to bring this fish to net.

Some minutes later, that's exactly where the permit ended up, his broad, silver side reflecting the morning sun like a mirror. My glee could not be contained, and I let out a whoop of delight. I'd begun to think that permit were uncatchable. Like John, this blind hog had finally found his acorn.

"Let's head east and look for a bonefish," Marshall suggested. He was trying his best to sound casual, but I knew, immediately, what he was thinking. I was thinking it, too: Grand Slam. With a permit on the board, I'd completed the most difficult of the three legs. Now, to land a bonefish and a tarpon before the sun melted into the Gulf of Mexico.

Easier said than done, of course. Three gorgeous flats and several fruitless hours later, I'd yet to cast to a bone. Marshall was nothing if not determined, though—even

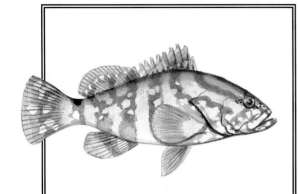

NASSAU GROUPER

Epinephelus striatus

More than any other grouper, the nassau is given to color variations, changing its striking patterns as easily as a cloud moves across the sun. A broad stripe from its eye to its dorsal is the most obvious feature of this often-hooked grouper, which averages eight to ten pounds.

if it meant showing Tom the hottest picks on the "buy list." On the fourth flat, we finally intercepted a nice bone. Marshall put me in perfect position, and the fish pounced on the fly. Then, it did a very unbonefishlike thing. Instead of bolting in the general direction of the Dry Tortugas, it leisurely swam a few yards and stopped, as if to ponder its alternatives. I was madly cranking the loose line onto the reel when the bone made up its mind. It took me deep into the backing, and a small eternity seemed to pass the fly line again. The bone fought hard, as bonefish always do, but it wound up in the net nevertheless. Like the permit, it was photographed, carefully revived, and released. Two down, one to go.

A thirty-five-minute boat ride brought us to the deep channel where John and I had jumped the tarpon the day before. Marshall poled slowly down the edge, scanning for the flash of rolling fish. He and Tom both spotted tarpon in the distance; the blind hog saw nothing. But when a fish rolled in the channel directly opposite the boat, I was ready. I'd exchanged the Scott for Marshall's heavy Sage tarpon rod, and after letting the fly sink for ten seconds I began retrieving it in slow, short strips, giving it action but keeping it down. When the line came tight, a tarpon in the fifty- to sixty-pound range catapulted skyward. The fish crashed back into the water, leaped again—and threw the hook. The second tarpon I had must have been taking notes, because it reprised the performance, breaking the point off the hook in the process.

Marshall tied on a new fly, and gently reminded me of the necessity of striking tarpon repeatedly once they're on the reel. (Driving a hook into a tarpon's mouth is about as easy as driving a hook in a metal bucket.) He also noted that for the Slam to count, I simply needed to get the butt of the leader through the rod tip. We would cross that bridge, however, when we came to it. Not to be outdone, the third tarpon rocketed out of the water like a Polaris missile and jettisoned the fly instantly. I was ready to eat nails. Time and tide were running out, and so, I feared, was my luck.

Activity in the channel began to slacken, and after a number of unrewarded casts I decided to speed up my retrieve. Wonder of wonders, the strategy worked. I struck the fish hard twice, got him on the reel and struck three more times. The hook held through a series of spectacular leaps, the tarpon haloed in glittering spray, but when at last I maneuvered the fish close my stomach fell. The fly was barely embedded in the corner of the tarpon's bony maw. Holding my breath, I applied as much side pressure as I dared. The line crawled through the guides inch by agonizing inch.

And then the butt of the leader passed through the rod tip. Marshall and Tom broke into boisterous applause, yelling, "Yeah! Slam! Alright!" The tarpon was close enough to gaff, but we had no intention of doing so. It was a moot point soon enough, for as I changed slightly the angle of pull, the hook slipped out. "That's the best release for the fish," Tom effused, "and the Slam counts."

I was numb. It honestly didn't seem real. The most I'd dared hope for was to finally catch a permit on a fly. And now I'd joined the handful of saltwater fly rodders who have achieved the Grand Slam of the flats. This wasn't just an acorn; it was an enormous, priceless truffle.

As we raced home in the slanting afternoon light, the water so thin that the hull seemed to be skimming over air, I couldn't help thinking about John. If his day at the office had been half as productive as my day on the flats, he'd be in the mood to celebrate, too.

A Day in May

from Just Before Dark

Jim Harrison

ITHOUT HAVING FLOWN OVER THIS PARTICU-lar stretch of water southwest of Key West, I can still envision it topographically: the infinite shadings of blue over the tidal flats—azure, indigo and the predominant light turquoise of the shallows with the paler striations of white sand. Then the brown turtle grass, the dark outlines of coral outcroppings or tidal cuts that game fish use to reach the feeding grounds, and the darker green random splotches of mangrove keys. Farther to the south is a sometimes garish penumbra of purple, that imaginary point where the Gulf and the Atlantic meet in a great ocean river, the Gulf Stream.

This vision is open to errant civilian pilots, gulls, frigate or man-o'-war birds at the edge of their northern cycle, and Navy pilots on practice bombing runs off the Marquesas. I saw it most poignantly last May, reflected off a motel wall in Hollywood after a month of butting my head into the movie industry with the kind of nondirectional energy that characterizes boobs from the Midwest. One evening I drove back to the room in a borrowed car, going eighty miles per hour, in wet underpants from the sort of poolside party I will refuse to remember on my deathbed. In no time at all I was on the red-eye flight from L.A. to Miami, where a friend picked me up at dawn. Before noon we reached Key West and launched the boat. Just a clean, bare skiff with no equipment save a saltwater fly rod and a box of tarpon flies. Already the baggage of the clumsy Hollywood hustle was fading; we pulled out of Garrison Bight, ran at thirty knots past Christmas Island, then slowed for the heavy riptide of the ship channel. It was hot, but I was somehow shivering. Off Mule Key, not an hour into it, the first tarpon was hooked, a single stray lying along a dark bank of turtle grass in cloudy light. It was a sloppy cast, but the hookup was good, with perhaps eighty pounds of fish thrashing upward in three shattering jumps before breaking off. The break off was fine because it was the beauty of the jumps I was looking for, and we let all the tarpon free anyway.

Afterward I noticed my forearm was twitching from the electric strength of the fish. With the sun and heat and wave-lap against the boat, thinking became oddly cellular, not cranial. I'd learned again how badly the body wants to feel good.

On the way back to Key West we paused near the wreckage of a shrimp trawler. Here, a few years back, we saw an explosion up on the flat and checked it out. It was a hammerhead shark, nearly as long as the seventeen-foot skiff, chasing tarpon in the shallow water. He paused to investigate us and we teased him with the push pole. The shark circled the skiff with one goggle eye raised and tried to figure out if we were a meal. There was a stiff wind, and the sun focused him in brilliant flashes under the swiftly fleeting clouds. The water only intermittently covered him, and his long, thick gray body glistened in a bulbous wake. Aside from a mostly imaginary threat, I could no more kill one of these creatures than I would a house pet. He belongs where he is and we are only visitors.

The next day was a long relaxing blank after the harsh, grisly nightlife that Key West specializes in—or that I seem to specialize in when I go to Key West. At dawn you always study the palm trees out the window. If they're merely rustling, the weather will be fine for fishing. If the palms are wild and bending in the wind, you check to see if anyone's in bed with you and, if not, you usually decide to make the run in bad weather. Once I fished thirty days in a row, celebrated God knows

HAMMERHEAD SHARK

Sphyrna mokarran

You won't forget your first great hammerhead. These are among the ultimate predators and followers of tarpon migrations. The largest, taken in Boca Grande Channel off the Marquesas, have topped one thousand pounds. If you fish for tarpon in these waters, you will meet Mr. Hammerhead. Be careful!

what most of every night, and took a whole month in Michigan to recover from the "vacation."

But a blank day on the flats can be a wonderful thing. The long hot hours of nothing are alleviated symmetrically by long hours of talking about food and other pleasures. It is a natural sauna that soothes the muscles and makes you grasp neurotically for the memory of whatever it was that drove you batty. Sometimes we dive into a reef to gig lobsters for dinner. Or stalk Cottrell Key, a strange combine rookery of frigatebirds and brown pelicans, hundreds of each filling the sky while the females stick glaring and restive to their nests. The air and still water of the lee are permeated by a hot low-tide smell of bird dung and the unearthly noise of the birds getting used to your presence. Later, you tie long gaudy flies to wire leaders and play with the barracuda off Cottrell, the tarpon having evidently fled to Tibet for the afternoon.

Now, there's a little panic associated with the slow fishing. After a month of it, I'm always stuck with an Andersonville or Russian Front sort of homesickness that swells in the throat and can only be handled by getting there. On a final trip, in contempt of our luck, we made the long, thirty-mile run to the Marquesas, and found a kind of tarpon epiphany. We saw nearly two hundred fish drifting in from the west, from the direction of the Dry Tortugas—a dozen schools, darkish torpedo shapes against white sand. On the flight home I still heard the gill plates rattling from the tarpon that jumped lithely over the bow of the boat, his six-foot silvery length seeming to hang freeze-framed a few feet away.

And at home, finally, in northern Michigan, the world was full of the cool green pastels of spring. On the first morning back, I went mushroom hunting with my four-year-old daughter and noted that the shades of green equaled the multifoliate blues of the tidal flats I'd just left. I looked for morel mushrooms among the first fiddleheads and wild leeks. Anna is as good at mushroom hunting as I am, perhaps because she's three feet closer to the earth and not daydreaming.

SURPRISE AT THE MARQUESAS

Lefty Kreh

Y DAD DIED WHEN I WAS ONLY SIX YEARS old. With my two younger brothers, I grew up without a father, but the three of us enjoyed the outdoors of central Maryland. Our local rivers were full of fish and the fields and woods loaded with game. Joe Brooks, the most famous outdoor writer of that time, lived in Baltimore, not too far away. Joe and several others formed an organization intent on introducing young boys to fishing—especially fly fishing. The organization was called the Brotherhood of the Junglecock, and the members held an annual affair a few miles from my home at Thurmont, Maryland.

I had met Joe and he was to have a major effect on my career as an outdoor writer. I told him of my determination to really get into the outdoor writing field, so whenever he had time he would give me advice and help me in any way he could. If I had a second father, it was Joe.

I started writing outdoor columns in 1951 or '52 (can't remember that far back). At the time there were almost no outdoor writers and as best I could remember, there were only four magazines devoted to the outdoors: *Outdoor Life, Field & Stream, Sports Afield,* and *Fur, Fish and Game.* By the mid-1950s I was writing for all of them and with Joe's advice, becoming a professional. I'll never be able to thank him for all that he did.

Then, in the summer of 1964, he called me and asked, "How would you like to be the manager of the MET tournament?"

127

I had no idea what he was talking about and replied, "What in the world is the MET tournament?"

Joe answered, "It's based in Miami and it's the largest fishing tournament in the world. It has trophies for catches of every kind of fish, from bluegills to blue marlin. I think it would be a great opportunity. Are you interested?"

With a little more discussion I agreed to try for the position, and was lucky enough to land it. I moved my wife, Ev, my son, Larry, and daughter, Vicky, to Miami. Of course, I wanted to try all of the fabulous fishing I had read about. I studied charts and talked to knowledgeable fishermen like Vic Dunaway, who at the time was outdoor editor of the *Miami Herald.*

After a number of exploratory trips, I determined that the two places that were least fished in southern Florida were the Content Keys and the Marquesas Islands. You have to remember that this was the mid-1960s. Flats boats as we know them today had not yet been developed. Motors that could run through grass or be tilted under power were undreamed of. For that reason, most people (guides included) fished mainly near their home docks.

I had a Boston Whaler. It was the smallest one they made, which I think was about thirteen feet. My son and I determined we would learn everything we could about those two places. In those days, the Lower Keys were paradise.

How deserted were the Marquesas when we started fishing there? Let me give you two examples. Larry and I broke down one afternoon near Mooney Harbor Key. Luckily, we had aboard plenty of water (melted ice in the cooler) and ample food. I poled the boat outside the Key hoping to catch somebody who might pass by. A day and half later a Cuban lobster fisherman came along and towed us into Key West. That is how few people fished there in the mid-1960s.

The Marquesas are a loosely formed group of keys in the shape of a wedding

"EDGE OF THE CHANNEL" *Peter Corbin*

JOLTHEAD PORGY

Calamus bajonado

Debates about the finest eating fish found in the Lower Keys most often nominate this porgy as the overall winner, especially among knowledgeable anglers. It is also a fine fighter and will sometimes eat a fly. A five-pounder will give you a battle you won't forget and a meal you'll always remember.

band, with breaks and openings in the circle. If you approach from the Key West side there is the East Channel that leads into the lake area in the center of the atoll. Larry and I quickly learned that if you arrived very early in the morning, came in the channel mouth, shut down the motor, and poled into the lake, you often discovered magic.

On those quiet mornings, especially during spring tides in the summer months, the lake near the channel was a bedroom for tarpon and permit. Hundreds of those fish (many very large) would be sleeping so close to the surface that the tips of their dorsal and tail fins showed above the water, like a great line of picket fence tops. Even then the fish were spooky, but you could always hook the first one. Then all hell broke loose as those hundreds of other fish fled the scene.

In about 1967, Larry and I were on our way back to the Marquesas. We arrived at the Boca Grande Channel just after dawn and found it as calm as a beaver pond. We sped across in our little Whaler and approached the entrance to the East Channel, which extends several hundred yards from the mangrove shoreline. There is quite a flat on the north side, and during higher spring tides it often holds small tarpon, some monster permit and is the only place in the area where I have seen bonefish.

On that morning when we were within three hundred yards of the flat, we could see a jet of water that looked like a six-foot-high fountain. But, the fountain was moving—rapidly. And, there were two other fountains! I wondered what in the hell was happening. We were within a hundred yards of those geysers when we finally understood.

Three huge hammerhead sharks were chasing twenty-five- to sixty-pound tarpon around the flat. These sharks were at least sixteen feet long and they reminded me of smallmouth bass chasing minnows around a river grass-bed. The frantic tarpon were darting, twisting and turning to avoid those terrible jaws. I couldn't believe how swiftly the sharks could move. One caught a tarpon of about forty pounds and the foaming water was discolored with a huge bloodstain.

Another shark came in our direction, and I understood where those fountains had come from. Those huge hammerheads had high dorsal fins that appeared to be rigid. When the sharks surged forward, chasing tarpon, water rushed against the wide, stiff dorsal fin, pushed up and out. They were the fountains jetting at least six feet in the air!

One hammerhead, after a tarpon, came within ten feet of our Whaler. I realized the monster was considerably bigger than our boat so I started the motor and we got out of there.

I have often heard the expression "nature in the raw," and it's still the only description I have for that memorable scene.

ANGLE OF ATTACK

Alan Farago

I T WAS HEAVY WORK KEEPING THE SKIFF POINTED INTO THE WIND. HARRY, THE guide, held us fast to this patch of Florida Bay, sixteen inches deep, whipped black and rippled flat with white-flecked windrows. Lightning lit Harry's face as he struggled from the poling platform aft to counter the violent gusts. I knelt at the bow to let the gale howl over me, holding my rod tip dead into the gale so the whole kit wouldn't sail off like a piece of paper.

All our attention was riveted ten feet ahead. There, the scythe tail of a sixty-pound permit waved out of the water, content below the fury; crushers buried in the sand.

My line was tipped with a 4.0 hook buried in a crablike scrap of brown shag carpet and weighted with two eyes the size of driveway gravel. I'd need every ounce. There would be no second chance.

The mark of a great fisherman is to always know the time. Time on a bright flawless day with fish tailing in shallow water, time to begin the false cast as the target turns its eyes away. Time on a day grim and overcast, fish hidden over dark bottom, time for the quick roll cast in dim light. And always time to wait, wait for that second to show the target the fly when it wants to eat, that single moment when the fish attacks, undeflected by thought or doubt.

I stood joyfully, my cheeks hollowed flat by the gale. My backcast nearly sheared off Harry's left ear. He ducked, and a bolt of lightning knocked him off the platform, which was good because my forward cast would have taken his head off.

It was the best cast I'd ever made into forty-five knots of wind. The permit ripped into the fly; I set the hook and stepped off the deck into the warm water. The skiff blew off into Northwest Channel. The last I saw of my guide, the top of his head was smoking . . .

132

"FIRST RUN" *Peter Corbin*

It is not true that all fishermen are liars. All listeners are dreamers. I would like to dream with you a story about fly fishing off Key West, of narwhals and waterspouts spinning bonefish out the sides, but since this is my first story about fishing, it is only appropriate to start at the beginning.

In the beginning there was shrimp. This is to say, to our uninitiated readers but especially those aesthetes who would rather blow their nose in a stranger's handkerchief than cast a fly tied by another's hand, there is no shame in live bait.

The hook is baited in the following manner. First, the tail of the shrimp is snapped or pinched between thumbnail and forefinger or bitten and tossed or spit over the side of the skiff. The barb end of the hook enters the business end of the shrimp. The hook is not pushed into the shrimp. This is a popular assumption and a wrong one. Similar misconceptions accompany our election of politicians into office. The shrimp is pushed onto the hook, gently bending the curvature of the shell to the bend of the hook the same way the best intentions of politicians are transformed by the pressures of the office. At the last as the shrimp head slides to the eyelet, the body is twisted 180 degrees so the barb will pierce, then exit, not through soft belly but its crustaceous back, pink and bubbling translucence. Now the shrimp is attractively hooked, legs all aflutter like a man stuck in a dismal career.

I first fished tarpon in the spring of 1978, years away from picking up a fly rod. March in Florida Bay. Never mind where. Focus on the young man of twenty-four, newly married, ascendant in manufacturing. His father introduces him to flats fishing. On one of those brilliant days that make bonefish stupid for no clear reason, the prodigal son feels the spinning reel scream in his hands and is hooked. Later, basking in the glow of his first saltwater conquest, he reflects on the power of the seven-pound fish and resolves to catch a hundred-seventy-pound monster in three feet of water. He will do it himself, with a trusty guide, and sets out the preparation, travel arrangements, and confirming phone calls toward an independent crusade for Key West, the Byzantium of tarpon.

Months later, the day has arrived. Harry, the guide, and I are at the gas dock at Garrison Bight Marina. The skiff bobs on greasy wavelets. Flush with fuel and shrimp, we pull away from land and everything that is familiar. The outboard backwash churns Victorian patterns of flotsam into a maelstrom. Now the excitement of starting out, the strangeness, the anticipation of watery wilderness, the good cheer as lunch is stowed away and wallet safely put up, snug and tight, all abate, subsiding in queasy indifference. Even at dawn, the tropics are sucking all the air out of the day.

In the morning Harry tries several spots, looking for tailing fish in the early light. I stand at the bow, following his instructions like a beagle. It will take time to cut the shape. Meanwhile I look the part: alert, ready, pointing. Using a fiberglass push pole to navigate the shallow flats, Harry searches for twenty or thirty minutes and, making a silent decision, startles me by jumping from platform to deck, clipping his push pole to the starboard rail, sparking the Yamaha to life and the skiff to a full plane within fifteen feet, all while I struggle to balance and remember, at the same time, whether the monofilament is wound at the reel by spinning the handle clockwise or counterclockwise.

The motion of the leaping boat throws me backward into my seat, onto the cushion next to Harry, who wordlessly navigates and fixes my line so the shrimp dangles with its friends in the bait well aft. Exactly where we are going is a mystery. The landscape is featureless. North, white-peaked cumulus pop up steeply, bottoms laden gray with moisture and flat as the Everglades. Every gradient of color is reflected in the mirror surface of the bay. I calm a nascent funk by noting the splendor of the full moon ghostly in the blue sky and doubt my guide is living the moment as I am.

This construct, that one must flow with the currents and the tide and be ever so

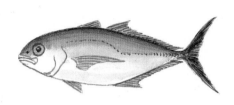

BLUE RUNNER

Caranx crysos

Unlike the crevalle, which can reach thirty pounds, the blue runner seldom tops two. Approaching a flat in your skiff, you will often meet a school of blue runners who will dart in silver showers, a living spray breaking at your bow. They will take flies, lures, even a bare hook. And broiled in their skin they are a tasty morsel.

careful not to let nautical competence dull one's sensitivity to the environment, gives me a sense of being Harry's equal to this business of life on the flats, and my plain happiness is reflected by Florida Bay itself, so calm we seem to float from one flat to the next, each more distant than the last, as though we are on a magic carpet until land drops off the horizon and we are the only living creatures left.

But this empty seascape, so vast it might prove the world is flat, slowly etches away my brash assumptions, leaving me feeling wan and dispirited. As morning progresses, no swirl of ray, no circling birds, no baitfish showering, no meandering shark enter our field of sight. For hours I stare down, over the rail, into seagrass meadows and bottom communities of sponges, sea fans, and soft corals still and motionless as a museum diorama.

By midmorning my fascination has dissolved like the clouds into the Gulf of Mexico. Everything is blinding blue and bright silver. Now the angle of sunlight prevents me from seeing more than a foot or two beyond the shallow water off the edge of the skiff. My new polarized glasses are useless. Woozy with lethargy, I watch my hooked shrimp trail from my rod tip, meandering in lazy circles on the surface of the water. Behind me, Harry seems to be moving with less than vigor, like a machine operator in midshift. I shift my weight in response to these disquieting feelings.

"Don't move the boat!" Harry hisses. "The fish can feel it." His words, shocking in the context of unfulfilled promises, prick me on the surly point of resentment. What fish? I mutter to myself, estrangement growing between us. The day was a stinker. My guide was a second-rate magician with a useless wand and no tricks up his sleeve. Now Harry drives the skiff to yet another flat. I question his judgment. Recriminations swirl in my mind. The engine's hydraulics lift the prop, a noise more damaging by far than the sound of my sneakers. Never mind. I hoist my rod and shrimp from the bait well, where at least it had friends to talk to even though they were all doomed, and mount the bow deck, resuming with insult what I had exalted before. It is at the moment of chastising myself for ever imagining this charade a crusade that Harry fairly shouts, "Look!"

Alarmed, I topple off the deck. Harry is pointing his push pole. I extend the angle of his gaze into the bay to calibrate my own, even though I am wearing a long-beaked cap.

"Floaters . . . see their tails?"

"Where?"

"There! There!"

"What are they?" I ask.

"Tarpon."

The word knots me.

Suddenly the world is right. We are guide and hunter now. Only I can't see what I'm looking for.

"There!" Harry points. "And there and there and there."

It had never occurred to me, in the months and hours leading up to this crusade, that we would find the Grail, but I wouldn't be able to see it. Now everything is wrong. My anxiety drives me wildly in another direction. I want to jump out of my skin.

Harry explodes. "Stop making so much noise! The fish can feel it! . . . Do you see them now?"

How to answer absorbs these seconds of concentration. My response should be tinged with earnest effort as a novice fisherman, good will as a human being, and modulated with a charter's admiration for the guide, a common courtesy I had withheld from Harry just one minute ago. How fortunate my discretion, through no fault of my own, in failing to give voice to these thoughts. How much more embarrassing

and difficult it would be to have assailed him with recriminations and now to respond with the only invention my reeling mind could conceive.

"What fish?" I whisper.

At certain times of the year, tarpon concentrate off Key West, and when the conditions are right, these prehistoric pelagics will stop and rest in shallow water against a bank or in a swale. Occasionally and only on the calmest days, tarpon will float at the surface, motionless as corks in a bowl of tap water.

Harry answers, in a voice timbered with awe, "They're everywhere."

Everywhere? And I see nothing, nothing but my pathetic performance now riddled with guilt and doubt.

"Get your rod ready!"

I fumble with the bail, making sure it is open, and close it and open it again to make sure it is not halfway closed but entirely open, hoping even if I get it wrong, the reel was made in Japan and has to work. But now the shrimp lies too far from the rod tip. I frantically shorten the lead, overwinding the shrimp into the top guide, and have to start the process all over again, unclasping the bail, losing grip on the line and watching the shrimp fall again.

Note this moment. You have achieved a level of success. School has come and gone. You have credit cards and bank accounts. You have slept with enough women to surmount the one fear that they are all your mother, and buried the fear that they're not. You are young and full of life. Your wife or significant other is not quite on to your game. And now, adrift on an undifferentiated sea of air and water, a fish so far out of water you don't know whether to breathe or hold your breath, your guide, a person you have only known for hours, not days or months or years like your family, your friends, your loved ones, now this stranger, this fisherman, points you to a revelation you paid good money to experience: that the true core of your nature is incompetence.

GREAT WHITE HERON
Ardea herodias

The lower Keys are about the only place in the United States where you'll see the great white. An alabaster version of the great blue heron, the white's mangrove hummock rookeries off Key West are national refuges and are not to be disturbed. When you see this magnificent creature, you'll be grateful it survives.

Harry fires away at me. "See? See? See?"

I can't see the tarpon. The harder I look, the more I see of myself: Narcissus at the well. All around me the Gulf throws up images from its mirrored surface showing in unremitting detail I had succeeded in hooking this: a slimy, flapping, horrific version of myself.

And as I stand there, abject, the most amazing glory leaps vertiginously from the water so close I might have touched it; a hundred-pound tarpon all yellow and gold with sun in its scales sails by and spears itself back into the silver sea, leaving a trace of ripple.

Through its perfect trajectory a single, unblinking eye, black as polished onyx, seems to be watching me emerge from myself like a hatching worm. I have no time to reflect on whether I am transforming into a palolo worm or a piece of sea snot. We are into fish. All around me, black wisps rise above the surface, then sink below. Every so often the fins move in unison, as though stirred by a common breath. And perhaps they are stirred by a common breath. I am witnessing the work of God.

Crashing from despair to epiphany, back and forth like a freshly caught cobia in an ice chest, I nearly shout in triumph, "I see them!"

Harry is not impressed. He is distant, in a world of his own, or at least a world from which I am excluded. He seems almost Olympian on his poling platform. I need him. Never mind the tarpon; I am on a roll. My heart is pounding. In a flight of fantasy, I imagine my sighting a breakthrough conferring eligibility in that brotherhood of men who meet the ocean on its own terms and conquer—or, at least, a fraternity of two men in the Gulf of Mexico. Possessed by stealth and great wads of adrenaline, I cast all doubt aside and turn to my sole purpose: catching tarpon with live bait.

Yes, of course. Now the fins are everywhere, numberless tarpon in our midst. Forward. Behind us. Port and starboard. This drug, fishing on the flats, has me in its grip.

"I have two fish at two o'clock, forty feet."

"Where?"

"Thirty . . . twenty-five feet. Look." Harry points with his push pole. I look. Napoleon never stared across the English Channel with such intensity.

"We can't get too close. They'll feel us." Suddenly the water bursts, boiling furiously at my feet. I can feel Harry slacken.

"How big were they?" I ask.

"A-hundred-ten pounds. . . . alright, I have another pair of fish . . . ten o'clock. Forty feet. Wait. I have a better angle."

Harry spins the boat.

"Should I cast?" That fish will be mine.

"Wait! Can you see which way they're facing?"

"I can't see anything." My mouth is very dry.

"Fifteen feet. Right in front of you. Look!" I am not breathing. Out of the corner of my eye I notice the shrimp wriggling fiercely. Even the shrimp can see the tarpon.

"We're on top of them," Harry whispers plaintively. And indeed, as I squint myopically two dark shapes emerge like shadows, like beams waterlogged under the surface five feet from the boat. Now, with one swift, reckless motion I raise my rod and fling that fat and happy shrimp to its destiny. Harry and I watch its graceful flight, the sun on the monofilment like the wire of a guided missile. The shrimp crashes twenty feet beyond the target. The tarpon bolts in a swirl so nervous it doesn't raise a splash. Well. The shrimp is enormous. How could I cast such a pendulous weight?

"Here, you don't need that split shot." I hand the rod tip back to Harry on the platform, my pride in bloody bits. He waits. Seconds pass. I look up at him quizzically. "Retrieve your line," he says.

How stupid; the little knowledge I have of fishing is dissolving like salt in water. I spin the reel handle, and suddenly two more tarpon breach from opposite directions, sailing in graceful arcs toward each other like dolphins at Sea World. The handle falls off the reel, clattering to the deck. This is too much.

Harry removes the lead sinker, looks over the shrimp, tosses it back to the water, and rethreads the handle on the reel. Without a word, he returns to his station. At least he knows his. Maybe he is trying to give me space to gather my wits, but I feel slighted. Am I not worth propping up? I step back to the deck. My knees are weak. I need to compose myself. I need shade. I am filled with a need to make excuses. This need is the reason we are persecuted by the nonfishing public, quick to find blame in the mote of another's eye.

This is not confessional poetry. I offer these tidbits, this bait if you will, to help improve our readers by showing how humility is restored through a recreational activity. As in the instance one fine morning off the Marquesas, when I held out a purple fly tied by my guide, Jeffrey Cardenas, to a mammoth school of migrating tarpon. Happy, happy, happy ocean fish. All morning the fish had been eating. In a nearby skiff, another fine guide, Gil Drake, watched.

It wasn't planned. You can never plan a happy, hungry school of migrating tarpon off the Marquesas. But it was a sure thing. I could have underhanded the fly. I could have used my forefinger and flicked it off the edge of the deck like a bottle cap to hook a fish when I noticed Gil aiming a video camera. He was aiming it at me. As I began false-casting, the notion occurred to me of using this event to audition as the star host of a Saturday morning cable fishing show, and, counting my residuals before my presentation, I lost my loop, hit myself in the back of the head, and wrapped myself in the fly line like an overtaxed Chinese noodle thrower. The school swam by, unmolested and majestic. I have been mute in Gil's presence ever since.

Return with me for a moment to the image of the twin breaching tarpon forming an arc, inviting me as into a pantheon where on this day alone one can drift with quiet and purposeful direction through an ocean of dreams. The dorsal fins poke out everywhere.

"Harry," I whisper. "How many fish are there?"

"At least a thousand." Although his response touches me, I am at that moment preoccupied by rivulets of sweat dripping through sunscreen into my eyes. It is all happening too fast. Do I have time to take off my sunglasses and wipe away the smear? Should I ask Harry?

"Nine o'clock. A monster. Sixty feet." I panic; my eyes are stinging. I want Harry to help me. I want Harry to hold the rod. I want Harry to cast the bait.

"Thirty feet." I curse. The bay is as impenetrable as a bead of mercury.

"Fifteen feet." I am in despair.

"Point your rod. Left . . . left!" I cringe under the weight of Harry's voice. We are on a battleship. I am the gray barrel aiming to the gunner's commands. "Cast twenty feet."

I never pray. Praying, I raise my rod, and at the moment of release I see the torpedo: enormous, a green beast fat and long. Several impulses move me at once. I reason that my cast is too long by a boat length. Seeking to restore my self-esteem and avert the mistakes that have marred my day, I clamp down on the monofilament to arrest the shrimp's flight. And why not? If you cast too far and see a great bag of line in the air, why not try to do the right thing and bring it back? I jerk the rod as though I know what the right thing is. Harry cries, "No!" and a pile of monofilament sloughs off my reel in a tangled, impenetrable rat's nest.

At that instant I incorrectly assume that Harry is outraged about the guilty mess I have made of his tackle, but my work has successive consequences. By stopping the

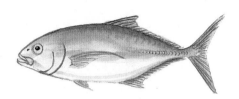

YELLOW JACK
Caranx bartholomaei

A yellow jack is precisely that: yellow. Traveling in the same circles as bar jack and blue runner, the yellow jack is equally feisty. Although it seldom tops three pounds, it is, pound for pound, as scrappy as its ubiquitous cousins. Just out of the water, its colors are breathtaking.

HAWKSBILL

Eretmocheyls imbricata imbricata

Not as large as the green turtle, the hawksbill is a look-alike cousin, and the two species have been known to hybridize. The source of tortoise shell ornaments and jewelry, this is a handsomely patterned, yellow-and-brown turtle you will find most often near coral reefs.

line and raising the rod, my intent was to put the shrimp in good position. But the shrimp, obeying higher laws, springs back as though on a bungee cord and lands with a loud *thwack* on the tarpon's head. Harry had anticipated this event. Perhaps it was even a part of his dream life. The tarpon bolts with the energy of a chrome fender slashing through the plate glass of a bank building.

"Let me change your shrimp," Harry says in a monotone that does not deny him the hope that a fresh bait could achieve better results than a new charter. I fume at his practiced, studied calm. Even if my cast had stunk, it was an insult insignificant in comparison to the guide's error that had allowed me, a paying customer, to drag a bait for so long that it looked like the last, lifeless floater in a tub of cocktail shrimp at a Shriners' convention. Harry had been too lazy to keep me armed with fresh and attractive shrimp. That's bait at the end of my line? I don't think so. That shrimp would not hunt, and it was not my fault.

"Next time, try leading the fish," Harry suggests. It was so fatuous, the way he tossed this kernel of fishing lore. Why hadn't he told me before I skulled the fish? The sun approaches the fattest hour of its day. The sweat pours off me. "You have to slide the shrimp in front of the tarpon's mouth. Not his tail." How irritating. You can't spank a fish to make it eat.

I knew that.

"And then let the shrimp drop. Just let it drop."

Finally, late in the afternoon, the odds turn up sevens my way. A miraculous cast pitches the bait seven feet beyond my target. My retrieve slides the shrimp seven inches in front of the tarpon's nose. I even stop a beat, to let the shrimp drop seven centimeters. My heart leaps, waiting for the strike. The tarpon farts a stream of seven bubbles—I count them—and in a final indignity sinks out of sight, not even bothering to flee. So you see, it is not true that all fishermen are liars.

What is true is that we are all dreamers. We listen to others' to gauge our own. My dreams are mottled, as though viewed underwater without a mask. Mostly they run from me like a pair of bonefish off the flats when I wake. Who knows why? The slap of the bay on the chine of the skiff. An arm raised. A pressure. A shadow.

When I stand on the deck of a flats skiff, staring through the skin of the bay, my quarry is as elusive as dreams and as obscure. I pole the flats to catch the wild part of me that will stick a hook in my flesh, the fish, to feel the lightness of being that comes with connection.

Such insights require the loosening of ligature, the waning of resiliency, of age that sticks us with reality that we pray is not too painful. The memory of spring once ours is cast through the length of the fly rod. Now it is easy to see through my younger self and even that self's odd dreams. It is easy to see how I arrived at fly fishing to express my tenuous hookup with the universe. The knots still hold.

That first day with tarpon, I was a threat to no one but myself. I fought a battle played to no one, generated no heat but my own in an ocean of possibility, viewed indifferently by Harry, who poled me from sleeping giant to sleeping giant, with the good manners of a croupier with the casino's favored comp. I suppose in Harry's eyes, the better judgment lay in pulling the player from the table, but it was not his.

At last, there are no more fish. The sun is falling through its lower quadrant. "Where have they all gone?" I ask. "I don't know. I'm not a fish." Harry jumps off his platform, stows his push pole, firing and lowering his engine at the same time.

There are some days, glorious as God can give us, when no angle of attack works. On such days the object of our desire becomes incandescent and disappears, like a sparkler after its final bright burn, leaving the imprint: a memory of the flame and a certainty that the object itself pales to our need for open sky, and an angle to see, to capture for a fleeting moment, what one dreams.

And of the lessons experience confers, take this one to the bank: On days when nothing moves but tarpon lazing at the surface off Key West, you'll do better with bare hands than live shrimp. You can't possibly catch a tarpon that way. Now fly fishing, that's another story.

ABOARD THE EDEN

from FAR TORTUGA

Peter Matthiessen

From the 1930s until 1972, tens of thousands of green turtles were commercially slaughtered for the market at the Key West turtle kraals at the foot of Margaret Street. Caught off the coast of Nicaragua and other turtle grounds in the Caribbean, the turtles supported a fishery that was a mainstay of the Lower Keys economy until the Endangered Species Act protected sea turtles in U.S. waters. Peter Matthiessen's novel Far Tortuga, *excerpted here, is the story of the last of the Caymanian turtle fishermen.*

THE ANCHOR LOOMS AND WASHES FREE. IN THE WHITE MARL sliding off the fluke, a polychaete worm, transparent, reflects a sun-spot in its blood; at the surface it writhes once and is snatched by a long houndfish, drawn by the roil in the harbor water.

Northeast trades, and casuarinas on the leeward strand, bent away into the west; over Prospect Church veer frigate birds on long black wings. Beyond Prospect, misted by sea spume, Bill Eden Point and Old Jones Bay sink away into the land.

The island turns.

The *Eden* passes from the lee into the white-capped stone-blue chop of the deep ocean.

A wash of white: a wave rises high on the port bow, hangs, slaps, collapses. Bright brown sargassum weed sails by, and a flying fish skips free of the bow, skidding away on thin clear wings into the blue oblivion.

To the west, migrating land birds, spinning north.

Raib replaces the canvas-and-lard baits with strips of flying fish. The silvery fish, attracted by the naked light over the engine hatch, have come aboard during the

147

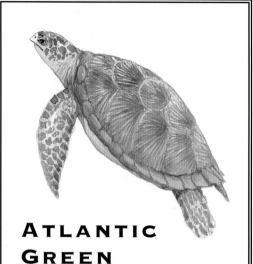

ATLANTIC GREEN TURTLE

Chelonia mydas mydas

Turtles will surprise you from time to time, surfacing near your boat. The green turtle is one you are least likely to see. Now endangered from past over-harvesting, these large (up to five hundred pounds) gentle creatures were caught and impounded at the Key West Turtle Kraals until 1972.

night. Squatting at the taffrail, he sews strips of fish to hooks with a sail needle, notching the baits to make them tail more naturally in the water. His thick hard lumpy fisherman's hands move gently, and though it is dead, he talks softly to the wild-eyed fish as if to calm it.

Fly too high, darlin, you fly too high.

He laughs his deep accumulating laugh, and his broad back quakes beneath the weathered shirt.

The *Eden* rides easily on the following wind, her jib and foresail taut. The trolling lines, hitched to the stanchions, sail out over the wake, and the baits, flashing at the surface, dart and hurry in the morning sea. Soon the fish rise; both lines go taut with a small *thump* and are hauled in hand over hand, skidding and cutting across the wake as the fish run.

Three kingfish, a Spanish mackerel, four barracuda fly up out of the sea; they slap and skitter on the deck. A barra with black spots and a black dorsal snaps at the bare legs and Athens smacks it with a marlin spike across the head. A glaze on the gelatin eyes: the pupil dims.

The catboat is rowed against the wind, from set to set—lone coral heads, narrow reef channels, round wells of white sand ringed by coral, called "white holes." Between sets, Raib rigs the next net to its buoy and clears the kelleck and the buoy line, so that it is ready to heave. With hands, toes and teeth, he spreads the whole length of the net to be sure it is hung properly and will not tangle, then heaves the kelleck on its line and throws the net out after it, using an overarm motion that casts the mesh wide in the air. One end of each net is secured to the log buoy of light wood, and this end is anchored by the kelleck. The net floats down the current like an underwater flag, shifting position with the change in tides: it is borne up by small floats along the surface line, and since the bottom is not weighted it hangs in the current at an angle. With its wide mesh, the light net encourages tangling yet permits the turtle to haul it to the surface when it has to breathe.

In the western light, the coral glows, fire. A shark glides outward from the dark wall, then accelerates with a stroke of its huge caudal. Further on, bonita crisscross, chasing bait fish; where the bonita chop the surface, the minnows spray into the air in silver showers, all across the sunlit coral.

The sprays of bait fish, catching the sun, have drawn the hunting terns, which beat along against the wind, just overhead. Fish and birds chase back and forth across the catboat's bow, the tern shriek lost in the cavernous booming on the reef.

The nets trail downwind from the reef, the float lines bunched up here and there in a rude tangle; the turtles thrash and sigh. As the catboat comes up on the net, the creatures sound, dragging the floats beneath the sea, but they are tired and soon surface.

Raib hooks the net with a small grapnel and hauls it in. Each crewman seizes a fore flipper of the turtle. They hoist it upright, facing away from the boat, then haul it on its back over the gunwales. It rests on the thwart until freed of the net, then is lowered, still upside down, into the bilges.

There are five green turtle in the net, each one two hundred pounds or more, and the broad calipees of bamboo yellow cover the bottom of the catboat. When first taken aboard, the turtles slap their flippers on their bellies; soon they lie still.

The catboat drifts down on the last net, which floats on the surface in a snarl. The huge loggerhead is wound inside it, wound so tightly that it cannot sound as the catboat nears; its small eye glowers through the netting. It is dragged into the catboat to be disentangled, and soon the massive head is freed, but the taut net and the beast's great weight make the job difficult in the small boat. The men move gingerly around the head, with its pink warty neck.

One by one, the turtles are hoisted from the catboats by means of a bridle secured to the bases of the fore flippers. Suspended from the tackle at the tip of the foremast boom, they are swung inboard over the rails. Athens grabs the heavy tail of a hanging male, to steady it, then pierces its flippers with a red poker brought from the fire in the galley stove: a hissing sound and a quick sweet stink of flesh. The turtle blinks. Then it is lowered to the deck, where palm thongs are run through the flipper holes, and the flippers are lashed tight across the belly.

Wodie slides the turtles aft, into the shade of the starboard companionway. Since they will be transferred to a crawl at Miskito Cay, they are left abovedecks. To keep them from sliding on the rough seas, Wodie kicks wedges under the shells and a wood pillow is placed beneath each head, which would otherwise hang back unsupported.

Parting the water, the great mantas catapult into the sky, spinning white bellies to the sun—black, white, white, black. Slowly they fall into the sea. In the windlessness the falls resound from the horizons.

Near the silent boat, a solitary ray rolls over and over in backward arcs, wings rippling, white belly with its eye-like gills revolving slowly just beneath the surface.

Twin wing tips part the leaden surface, holding a moment as if listening. Then water raises softly and is still.

A broken sky.

Strings of ibis and egrets, bone white, turn pale pink as they cross a broken sunset.

The boat drifts down the river in soft rain.

A school of mullet, parted, sprays the surface; a heron quawks once, passing over, under a hidden moon.

At the delta, the catboat is hauled across salt wavelets on the bar and launched into the surf. There are no stars; the sea and shore are dark. Raib has taken a range on the way in, using the islet point and a great stump; adjusting his heading, he glances back every few moments down the straight line of his wake.

Rain pocks on the night sea.

A masthead light, blurred by the rain.

LITTLE BLUE HERON

Egretta caerulea

For many years, one of these small, slate-blue herons found its daily seafood ration at the Garrison Bight Marina in Key West. Like pelicans and some of the egrets, little blues have learned how to coexist with anglers. You can, however, find them in the wild every now and then.

CASTING FOR TARPON

Nelson Bryant

LY FISHING FOR TARPON IS NOT FOR THOSE WHO SEEK TO blend angling with sweet sessions of silent thought. It is, if done properly, an intense hunt culminating in the few seconds when one's offering must be properly presented to the gray shapes moving past. Often there is only time for one cast and if that is botched the fish will either not see the fly or hurtle away in terror if it lands too close.

And when, as often happens, not many fish are seen, one must also battle boredom, hour after hour of inactivity while standing in the bow of a shallow-draft, outboard-powered skiff, fly rod in hand as the guide on his elevated platform in the stern poles across miles of shallow, shimmering flats. It may also involve a stakeout on the edge of a deep channel in the flats that tarpon are wont to use.

When the intervals between tarpon sightings last an hour or more, an angler's self-discipline is sorely tested. The sun and the motion of the boat are soporific and he looks ahead but does not see, and at such a time the guide's shout that he has spotted a fish may find the angler totally unprepared to go swiftly into action. He will discover that he is standing on one of the loose coils of his fly line or, in a frenetic response to the guide's exhortation to "Cast! For God's sake, cast!" he may deliver the fly to the wrong end of the fish.

It is a highly specialized form of angling for those who wish to go after one of the world's most highly prized game fishes in the most difficult manner possible.

For the first three hours after Roger Donald of Brooklyn and I set forth from Key West, we saw no tarpon even though Captain Harry Spear, our intense and

accomplished light tackle guide who is particularly fond of fly fishing, had poled steadily most of that time.

Our captain was not depressed, however, for he had been saving what he felt would be the most promising area—the Marquesas Keys, which are a few miles west of Key West—for late in the afternoon. He had delayed taking us there because many of the anglers and guides involved in a Florida Keys tarpon-fishing tournament would be working the area until the competition's 4 P.M. curfew.

The last tournament boat was leaving when we arrived. I was admiring a lone coconut palm towering above the green mangroves on the desolate beach before me when Captain Spear shouted that four tarpon were swimming directly at me. I began my cast before I saw them—most occasional tarpon anglers, and I am no exception, have trouble spotting tarpon—but the fly was on the mark. I had made only two six-inch retrieves when one of the fish hit. I struck back hard, three times, and a glorious silvery shape erupted from the pale green water. I remembered to "bow," to lower the rod and shove it toward the fish, thus creating as much slack line as possible, a maneuver that lessens the chance of a broken leader.

The next critical phase of fly fishing for tarpon—"getting the fish on the reel"—was accomplished without mishap. The loose coils of fly line lying on the deck must go through the rod's guides without snarling as the fish makes its initial run.

Although what follows is hard work, it is marvelously satisfying. The fish, which will probably jump three or four more times, is linked with the angler, and all the latter has to do is to constantly maintain all the pressure his tackle can stand.

Ten minutes and four more jumps after my tarpon was hooked, Captain Spear announced that I would have to put more heat on the fish—we estimated its weight at eighty to ninety pounds—if we were to have time to try for another.

"THUNDER AND LIGHTNING" *Peter Corbin*

Fifteen minutes after the struggle began, when I had the tarpon wallowing about the boat less than two rods lengths away, the leader—which had been frayed by contact with the fish—parted. That—and it is one of the peculiar charms of tarpon angling—was of no concern to any of us. Had the fish been brought to the boat it would have been released. Very few of today's anglers—fly fishermen in particular—kill a tarpon unless there is a possibility it is a record catch. The largest tarpon taken on a fly rod—caught in 1982 off Homosassa, Florida—weighed 188 pounds. We saw several more tarpon among the Marquesas but none was within casting range.

That night a nasty east wind was born, making it impossible to revisit—in the two days of angling remaining to Mr. Donald and me—the Marquesas, and fruitless to attempt any extensive poling on the flats.

We spent those two days staked out on the edge of a lovely green hole in the oceanside flats a few miles east of Key West. Our guide chose the spot because he knew that tarpon were wont to visit it and because its white sand bottom would make it easier for my companion and me to see the fish approaching. We did rather well in that location, hooking and jumping four more tarpon, all between seventy and eighty pounds, and bringing one to the boat.

The last-mentioned fish was caught by Captain Spear under rather bizarre circumstances. No tarpon had been spotted for an hour and just for something to do I asked him if I could see how one of his big fly rods performed. I made a long cast out into a deep portion of the aforementioned hole, remarking that I liked the way the rod handled, and passed it to him with the fly still in the water. He had retrieved the fly no more than three feet when a tarpon hit, jumped, and raced 150 yards out into the ocean before launching high above the white caps in a shower of wind-torn spray.

Tarpon are unpredictable creatures. Earlier in the day, after a series of them had refused—even fled from—our flies, one took a shrimp-baited hook and then went to pick up a fly. For a moment, he was on two rods simultaneously.

The morning Mr. Donald and I left the Keys, the harassing wind had died to a whisper, which is why, if one has the time and the money, one should set aside more days than we did for pursuing *Megalops atlantica.*

BRIDGE LINES AND PALS

Flip Pallot

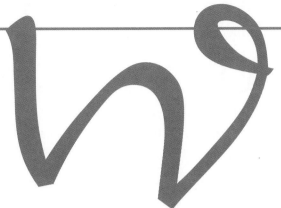

HAT GREAT GOOD FORTUNE TO HAVE BEEN born and have grown up in South Florida at a moment in time when the game of saltwater fly fishing was just beginning to be played.

Unfortunately, at that time, I was pretty young, very avid, but not a very serious player in the new game.

My closest friends, John Emery, Norman Duncan, and Chico Fernandez, were in the same boat as I was, and that was . . . no boat at all!

We did, however, have access to one or another of our parents' automobiles, and our favorite outing was to drive to several of the many bridges along the lower Florida Keys and fish off the bridges for giant tarpon at night.

The tarpon would lie in the shadow of the bridge on the up-current side. Here they would face into the swift current waiting to ambush crabs, mullet, shrimp, and other hapless creatures that make up the varied diet of *Megalops atlantica*.

My recollection is that in those days (the late fifties and early sixties), a fly line cost about fourteen dollars. Between the four of us, most of the time, we never had fourteen dollars, but somehow we always had fly lines. The fourteen-dollar line of choice back then was a Shakespeare GAAF, or 9-weight by today's measure. Our method was basic; one of us would stand on the edge of the bridge span, backcast between speeding traffic, and launch a chicken-sized fly up-current of the tarpon as they lay in the shadow of the bridge.

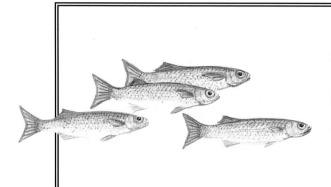

STRIPED MULLET

Mugil cephalus

One of the tarpon's favorite snacks, mullet will travel into brackish and fresh water. Often in small schools around the docks in Key West's Garrison Bight, blunt-headed, blue-gray mullet will swim in perfect circles until a seabird's shadow sends them scattering in a rattle of white water.

Most of the times as the fly washed over the suspended tarpon they would rise like giant brown trout, flash in the dim light of the bridge, and inhale the fly.

That moment was like attaching two hundred volts to a young boy's heart. I can still see those strikes in my mind's eye, and feel the voltage as though it were five minutes ago.

I know that Chico, Norman, and "Little" John felt the same voltage, as it was the constant subject of conversation on the three-hour ride home from the Lower Keys.

The bad part of this method of tarpon fishing was that once you successfully hooked a bridge tarpon, you could count on a few mind-boggling jumps, but then, inevitably, the tarpon would swim through the bridge, cutting your backing as he or she (the really big ones were always shes) went through the pilings under the bridge.

We never mourned the loss of a tarpon regardless of the size. As a matter of fact, never actually catching one allowed us to estimate their size in the wildest ways.

It was the loss of the fly lines that sent us into financial shock. Each lost line had to be replaced by lots of hard work to earn enough to replace it.

It was after a particularly great May night of tarpon fishing, when there was not a fly line left among us, that someone in the group had an epiphany . . . bridge lines!

Norman Duncan's garage in the village of Coconut Grove was our fishing headquarters. It was in Norman's garage that some of our wildest ideas were born. It was where we built our rods, tied our flies, and wound thousands of yards of backing on our combined collection of Pflueger Medalist fly reels. It was in Norman Duncan's garage that bridge lines were born.

The basic concept involved a GAAF fly line strung between trees behind the garage. Alongside the fly line we would string a single section of five-hundred-pound-test monafilament. Using emery paper, we duplicated the exact taper of the GAAF line on the strand of five-hundred-pound-test mono . . . bridge line!

It mattered not one whit that this new line was so stiff that it could not be wound onto a reel. It also mattered not that we knew of no good connection between bridge line and the leader butt-section. In our ignorance, it mattered not that it was weight, not taper, that determined the castability of fly line.

We simply wound the bridge lines into large coils, toted them out onto the bridges of the Lower Keys, and fished them as though Joe Brooks himself had designed them.

Bridge lines gave us new financial independence. All that money we saved on fly lines, and some better jobs, gave us the solvency to become partners in a boat (but that's another story). In time, we learned the dynamics of fly lines and in time our fingers were restored (from all the sanding on monofilament), and as I look back on those early days of saltwater fly fishing, I realize how much I miss . . . bridge lines and pals.

KEY WEST WITH CAPTAIN GIL DRAKE

Nathaniel P. Reed

For many years, Nathaniel P. Reed has kept detailed journals of each of his angling days, whether they've been on the Alta and the Namsen in Norway, the Moisie in Quebec, the Tweed in Scotland or the flats off Key West. No other day, however, is the equal of Sunday, March 5, 1989, when he fished with Captain Gil Drake out of Key West.

Saturday, March 4, 1989
Arrived in Key West in midafternoon.

Sunday, March 5
Blowing at twenty knots plus with a light cloud cover. A huge winter front was blowing into Florida.
At 8:30 A.M. Gil Drake and I changed leaders and then buzzed over to a nearby flat.

At 9:10 A.M., after several casts at mid-teen-sized permit, Gil turned the skiff skillfully, giving me a perfect shot at a large single permit. The permit stared at the epoxy fly, and when I twitched the fly off the bottom, to our great surprise, the permit seized it. After a spirited twelve-minute fight, Gil netted and we photographed a superb twenty-two-pound permit that then swam off, no worse for wear.

Oh, joy, oh, rapture: number five on a fly!

10:15 A.M. After a few tough casts that produced no interest, another large single permit was spotted taking a crab out of a floating mass of seaweed.

Again, a perfect stalk gave me a clean cast of some fifty-five feet. The permit turned slowly at the fly's splash—stared—and, as I tweaked the fly ever so gently, he lunged, taking it deeply in his throat. After a superb running flight, we landed a twenty-pounder and photographed it and released it. A double! Both big fish! Much jubilation.

160

The tide increased, and although permit were still occasionally visible we changed flats, heading out into the vast submerged flats between Key West and the Marquesa Islands.

We ate lunch and began slowly checking a good-looking bar.

At 1:10 P.M., we both spotted a large permit coming onto the flat. After a long, careful stalk, another good cast produced similar results. The permit slowly turned to the fly and, after I twitched it, dove onto it. The barbless hook was firmly set in his mouth's corner.

Off he went like an express train. The backing sang through the waters. Gil said, "Careful," so I fought him hard but with care. After twenty heart-rending minutes, he was ours—a huge permit in scale but a light one weighing twenty-five pounds.

This particular permit was one of those golden ones with a large patch of yellow on his stomach. He was as beautiful a fish as I have ever seen.

At 3:00 P.M., Gil moved me toward a pod of three smallish permit. As I worked the fly away from them, one charged. A tiny barracuda took the fly, and the permit vanished.

By 4:00 P.M., we could not find another permit and headed home. I joined a small group of three men who have landed three permit in one day, and the size of my three may well be a record.

Monday, March 6

The wind had dropped. The sky was covered with high level cirrus clouds and low cumulus. Visibility was terrible—the water looked milky from the sky's reflection.

There were permit all over the flat that Gil chose to start on: big ones and small ones, some small schools and loners.

Action was fast and furious—especially with the visibility such a limiting factor.

JEFFREY CARDENAS

The permit could see us, and they flushed from any movement—the boat, the guide, the angler, the fly line, and the fly. It was humbling, annoying, and finally, hilarious! We were brought back to the realities of permit fishing when we could see that they were simply the toughest fish to hook. We changed areas again—permit everywhere.

I finally had a small permit chase the fly—open his mouth—but I never made contact. Did he refuse it or did I pull it away from him?

We quit in the afternoon due to complete cloud cover and zero visibility.

Tuesday, March 7

The front arrived, drenching Key West with rainfall. I sat in Gil's living room and learned wonderful new knots and line loops.

The nail knot between the line and the backing, even beautifully tied, clangs out of the rod's guides. The loop system slides through easily. I finally learned the process of making the line loops and perfected the Bimini twist for the backing loop.

Linda complained that we looked like Cheshire cats! Smiles, broad smiles, graced our faces.

I am still on cloud nine!

WOODY

Guy de la Valdéne

une 8, 1969

Woody Sexton and I sat in the stern of his sixteen-foot Nova Scotia skiff waiting for the soft gray cloud that had chased and caught the morning sun to pass. The entire upper end of Coupon Bight was under the authority of that cloud, and there seemed little point in poling, so we waited—the engine idling, the bow barely pushing a wake—waited for the sun to escape, to undress the shadows and to expose the mysteries of the flats that lay ahead.

We had been fishing together for fifty-five days and the skiff had grown as confining as a glove. Down time and daily repetitions had elevated the smallest, most idiotic hint of humor to the level of jumping fish. I had been following a mosquito's windblown journey from the dock to the fishing grounds; now I watched it sink its stylet into Woody's neck.

"Goddamn bloodsucking son of a bitch," he said, jumping up. The skiff tipped to starboard. He took a shot at killing the insect with his hat, missed, and rambled on about malaria, dengue, yellow fever encephalitis and other insect-related diseases. Woody's forearms are knotted like a sailor's; his face, full of folds and crevasses. The mosquito headed for shore. Woody shoved the fishing hat back down on his short white hair.

My friend is a time bomb of encyclopedic knowledge that just about anything will set off. He uses words like *C. pipiens quinquefasciastus* for a house mosquito and *Lympho Granuloma Unganaly* instead of VD. We haven't known each other very long, a season, two at the most and so, when we aren't actively stalking fish (which is most of the time) we talk about medicine, about river systems, including ocean currents, about books by Roderick Haig Brown, bird migrations and bird-hunting, fly fishing and tools of all kinds from bait-casting reels to outboard engines. Woody gets bored easily and therefore reads a lot. He was born with a critical mind, a near perfect memory, and had graduated with a degree from Humboldt State University with the world at his feet. By then he knew the world to be too old in the ways of stupidity and corruption ever to be young again. A young whore with rotten teeth. Woody fled to the woods, where he lived in a medium of angles, fulcrums and danger. A world in which a man survives through his skills and judgment. He could have been a doctor or an engineer, but he chose instead to be a lumberman, a master lumberman.

I didn't tell Woody that I watched the mosquito bite him without warning, but said instead that the same humid weather that breeds mosquitoes was acting as a rallying call for tarpon, migrating in the folds of the Gulf Stream, to come ashore. The fishing had been good. We saw and hooked tarpon every day.

Woody relaxed his grip on the tiller and the skiff lost momentum. The sun struggled from under the pink underbelly of its guardian and light poured itself over the water. Heat fell down the sides of our faces. He stood and I sat, both of us watching for disturbances on the bright surface of Coupon Bight: for shapes inside shadows, for distortions in the oily rhythm of the tide, the motion, for rings, for surges of water escaping off the heads of big fish, of tarpon.

We'd both celebrated birthdays last month. I turned twenty-five, Woody forty-seven. He wasn't happy about it; I didn't care. His strength comes from having worked for twenty years in the redwood forests of California. Nowadays he toned up by twirling a cement block tied to a string around his body like a hammer thrower, for thirty minutes every morning before we go fishing. I am not nearly as strong but I am younger and played at most of the sports that wealthy children play.

I pulled sixty feet of fly line off the reel, stretched it and dropped it at my feet. Woody raised the forty-horsepower engine manually, unleashed the push pole from its chocks and stood in the bow.

His wooden skiff had been built in Islamorada from a Nova Scotia mold. It was light over the water, a dream to pole, wet and tippy because of its round chine. We had jumped almost two hundred tarpon from this navy-gray-colored skiff in the past fifty-five days.

Woody maneuvered us to the fishing grounds with conviction, a surge of water rising and falling with each push of the pole. We advanced with impudence into the sandier, shallower waters that girdle the north end of the bight. The big tarpon lay in the deeper grassy bottom to the west—sleeping like fat old men, inches above the bottom—but out of a sense of tradition, we always begin in the north corner: an enclave into which visiting schools of fish paint silvery shadows on a sand-colored bottom.

Woody poles with the same determination with which he bird hunts in Idaho. "I miss the smell of mountains," he said for the first time two weeks ago. It meant that his season in Florida was almost over. He now dreams of anadromous fish and mountain-climbing birds. In a week, or two at the most, he will fill the cab of his Ford pickup truck with his possessions and drive first to Northern California, where he'll hunt for housing in a small town with a good library, and later, to Idaho, where he'll fish for steelhead, carry a gun under the clouds and hunt for elegant birds and ponder the universe. An autumnal quest that defines Woody's ferocious resistance to mainstream America and the inevitable erosion of his freedom. Woody works as a Keys flats guide for five months of each year in order to spend the following seven free from the tepid minds of the population at large, his neighbors that are loud and fat, and his fellow anglers.

"I watched the entire side of a mountain talk and run uphill," he said, describing an October morning in 1964 when he pushed two thousand chukars into flight, from cheek grass to sage slope without a dog. Another morning in the Bryan Pool on the Eel River he landed five steelhead from twelve, up to eighteen, pounds on a Polar shrimp fly; bright, strong fish, perfect hosts to the sea lice they carried to the river bank. Woody doesn't exaggerate about anything. In fact, his weight estimate of the tarpon is as low as mine. Neither of us sees the point in deluding ourselves. We leave that to the amateurs and to those who write about fishing for a living and who, for the sake of survival, feel impelled to impress.

Woody came to the Keys in 1959 from the rivers of California, the Mad, the Eel, the Trinity, the Klamath, the Smith, where he and other young men of his generation braved chest-deep, cold water for a chance at sea-run fish; men who did what it took to present a fly properly, including hurling 600-grain lead-core shooting heads into heavy water from dawn to dusk. And like gods, after a few years these men became part of the rivers they fished just like mariners become the tide they sail.

In terms of making the throw, the Westerners are light-years ahead of us Floridians and once they adapt to the wind and the converging angles of fish and boat, the mechanics of casting a fly while standing on top of the water rather than in it are ordinary. Fly fishing, like all sports, is about angles—stationary ones and moving ones— billiards versus soccer. The warm climate, the shallow saltwater and the fish—particularly the tarpon—drew Woody and his peers south much as gold drew their forefathers west.

"In those days," Woody said, "during a spring tide, one expected to see five, six, maybe seven hundred fish in Coupon Bight. Now, the boat traffic and the commercial real estate development is such, we're lucky if we see fifty." He cupped the palm of his right hand around his sunglasses and peered into the water from under the bill of

"THE FLATS FISHERMAN" *Peter Corbin*

his hat. With a touch of melancholy he added, "That first year my partner, Jim Adams, and I used Fisher blanks and Jimmy Green fly rods, Hardy and Young reels and threw shooting heads at tarpon. We fished out of a twelve-foot aluminum boat powered by a seven-horsepower engine and poled with a borrowed curtain rod. We didn't know much except that fish have to eat. We applied ourselves to what we knew and made the casts. It made good adventure and we jumped one hell of a lot of tarpon."

Woody, like anyone who spends the better part of his life alone, gets agitated when he talks about natural matters that thanks to man's interference are disappearing. "Politicians and lawyers set the rules and multiply like rats." Woody is introducing me, little by little, to man's obligation to nature. My sporting life before meeting him was European by birthright, which basically translates into blasting everything that moves. My new fishing friend, my mentor and teacher, is more interested in the ways of crows than in the ways of men.

"Fish!" Woody pointed to a disturbance one hundred yards down-light. He wedged the pole against his hip and spun the stern of the skiff toward the commotion. The abnormalities of disturbed water were evident. The flat rippled as if pushed over boulders. A moment later, sunlight painted the chiseled head of fish the color of bronze.

"Ten, maybe fifteen tarpon, coming at us," he said.

I rolled out thirty feet of fly line, clearing it of a memory that sometimes impels it to wrap itself around my foot. The orange and yellow fly, tied to be fished in dark water, returned wet and slick as a worm. I left a measure of slack in the line and held the shank of the hook between the fingers of my left hand. It was dead calm and one by one the tarpon surfaced, some somber, some with purpose, and others playful; all causing the sea to part and all causing concern within the school. I caught myself rocking my right wrist back and forth, back and forth, forcing the belly of the line to roll and pull against the fly.

Some of the oldest-looking fish in the world swam into range and any sensible notion of time disappeared. I heard the rub of hands against the fiberglass and felt the skiff yaw to the right. A window of sky opened and out of habit, I sidearmed my backcast through it and drove the fly low over the water under the nonexistent wind. The fly landed where it was meant to, a leader's length beyond and in front of the school. A big mouth, cavernous as a chimney, rose out of the water and opened. I struck, but I struck too soon and my offering sailed gracefully through the air, falling on top of a melancholic tangle of fly line.

"Shit! Shit and shit," I howled at the huge puckers of creamy water the tarpon left in their hurry to depart. I have a tendency to pull hooks out of fishes' mouths. I have been doing it with a distressing regularity since I first started to fly-fish in 1966.

"Shit!" I said again. Woody smiled and said nothing.

I poled and Woody fished. That's our deal. Thirty bucks a day, we share the fishing and I bring lunch. His regular fee is sixty dollars.

At times, we trailer his skiff and look for fish below Key West, but the lower Keys is where Woody is comfortable: Big Pine Key, Sumerland, Cudjoe, the Seven Mile Bridge during the palolo worm hatch, Monster Point, and the Eccentrics, where tarpon swim out of deep channels looking like thick black eels.

Our best fishing takes place in and around Loggerhead, where earlier in the spring I cast at one of the oldest tarpon in the world finning like a trout against the current at the head of the first channel below Hommel's Corner. A fish so huge it looked like a 350-pound boar-hog with seaweed growing out of its gills. I drifted my fly—a morsel the size of a plankton—inches in front of its maw three times, but the giant acknowledged neither it nor us and simply swam away.

ROYAL TERN

Sterna maxima

A large, slim, dramatic tern with a high-pitched call, the royal tern sports a deeply forked tail and a black crest in the summer. The most graceful of the waterbirds, terns hover and dive for fish, thrilling you with the effortless rhythms of their airy flight.

In the mornings I drive from Key West to Big Pine Key. The first rays of light glance off the blacktop. In the afternoons it is a tougher drive because the sun sits higher in the windshield and because my eyes are tired from probing through layers of sea, and overloaded from the incongruity of watching great big fish fly across the sky. Willie Mae, my housekeeper, greets me with a drink on the doorstep of the Conch house on Duval Street my wife and I rent each spring. Willie Mae is a large and reassuring woman with shiny black skin, a permanent smile and a gift for making chicken sandwiches. She tolerates my wife but loves me, which makes for delicious excesses of solicitude. Whenever I want sympathy, I overstate the hardships of a sportsman's life.

Woody has the high casting motion of the deep river-wader. On the backcast, his hands hug his right ear. His double haul is concise and powerful. He is a master of the short cast—which doesn't mean Woody can't snap the backing against the reel any time he feels like it—and is at his best when he sees fish late and makes the throw purely from instinct. A long string of rolling tarpon, noodling up to the boat, turns into an intellectual conundrum, much like worrying about where to lead a duck passing across the seamless backdrop of a bluebird sky. Woody snaps his casts; I like to shoot a gun.

I poled the north side of Coupon Bight, the rising sun warm on my back. The turtle grass eight feet below the hull leaned with the tide. Coral heads scattered like dominoes poked out of the bottom, adding to the difficulty of poling. For the sake of silence (the clang of a pole's hardwood foot hitting rock shatters the nerves of large, sleeping fish), I could not drive my downstroke with the speed I would have liked; instead, I had to catch the pole before it reached the bottom and ease into the grass. My hands hydroplaned on a permanent film of water. The powerstroke ended at my knees.

Two tarpon swam parallel to the boat, deep, dark shapes passing. Woody made a quick half-moon cast behind his right shoulder and hammered the rod forward, stopping it short, as if hitting a wall. The fly turned over ten feet ahead of the closest fish, a hundred-pounder, followed by a much smaller male. The big female rose to the fly and was immediately knocked over by her companion. The light caught a confusion of silver bodies. Three large, round scales spun to the bottom.

A fifty-pound tarpon jumped cleanly out of the water close to the boat. I didn't know if it was hooked or simply jumping to get away. Much to-do about a two-inch meal, I thought, as I watched the fly exit, like magic, out of its mouth.

"I never struck him," Woody exclaimed. "But he sure hip-checked that big mother out of the way!"

"Again!" I said. A third tarpon, deep and hard to see, swam toward the skiff. Woody made the throw and let the fly sink. This time, something slow and confident rose from the grass, settled behind the fly, opened its mouth, and ate it. There was something about the size of the fish in relation to the fly, the boat and us that didn't fit the proportions of the tarpon we had been jumping; it was unsettling, like an untended door closing on a dark night. Woody held the rod low and horizontal to the water and struck the fish. The fiberglass blank bowed sharply and the ocean came alive as a tarpon as broad as the wing of a plane cartwheeled through the surface and into the sky thirty feet from the boat. A silverfish with golden eyes rose into the air, shedding coins of light, bending the scales of our imagination. At the apex of its jump, it hesitated for an instant, pinned by gravity, and tumbled like an anvil back to the sea. Yards of white water replaced it. The fly rod in Woody's hand looked ludicrous and small. We were speechless.

Again and again and again this dancer of a fish sailed through the warm humid air dripping with light and power. Woody turned, his eyes round under his sunglasses. "What do you think, two hundred pounds?" he asked.

I had the engine down and started. "At least," I answered. He turned away and we followed the fish. Each time Woody leaned from the waist the tarpon jumped.

And so it went: Eleven times the fish hurdled through the glasslike surface of Coupon Bight, eleven jumps into a foreign medium, eleven back-breaking vaults, and eleven back-breaking falls. The fish dragged us to the far side of the bight. Woody reeled. Sweat stained his shirt. I kept the fish to one side of the skiff, tried to outguess its moves and keep the slack out of the line. Woody worked the fly line back onto the reel. The giant rolled and jumped partially out of water. It shook its gill plates in exhausted irritation and when it fell, it fell slowly and lay on its side like a timbered tree, resting on a film of water, benumbed, the tips of its fins shivering.

Our only chance was to gaff the fish then and there. If the tarpon caught its second wind, we would be in for a grudge fight the twelve-pound-test leader would almost certainly loose. I idled the skiff as close as I dared and cut the engine, unwilling to disturb the tarpon's stupor. Woody reeled the weary fish closer to the skiff. It looked twelve feet long. I reached for the gaff we kept tethered to the gunnel and my heart sank.

"Woody! We left the damn thing on shore!"

We had both killed tarpon for others and hadn't liked it. We talked and agreed never to kill another one. A tarpon is too much like a St. Bernard, a generous fish with a massive heart, a fish with a past, a fish with a soul, and who, except for a fool, would deliberately kill a soul?

However, the fact was that neither of us had ever imagined that a tarpon fifty pounds heavier than the world record would one day lay within arm's reach of knaves like us. I rummaged in the bow and found the lip gaff.

"When I get it in its mouth, we'll pull him into the boat," I said, reaching over the side. The big fish dropped out of range. The tip of the rod touched the water. Slowly, carefully, Woody raised it. The fly rod bent and the fish moved. The odds

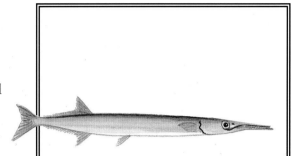

HOUNDFISH
Tylosurus crocodilus

Any sizable, long, lean, silver tubular fish you see leaping clear of shoal waters on the flats is almost certainly a houndfish. Most likely it's being chased by a barracuda. Houndfish can grow to five feet, and they do grab flies every now and then. Be careful of the teeth they were named for when you release them.

were against us. Even if I lip-gaffed it, we would probably turn the boat over trying to get him in. However, we knew we had to try, not for the killing or for the glory, but with finishing the job at hand.

I leaned over until my right arm was completely underwater. When the gaff glanced off the broad bony side of the tarpon's head, the fish's tail sent it back to the bottom. Once again Woody cajoled the tarpon back. This time though, the fish, perhaps waking from a dream, sensed our unholy presence and resisted. Woody applied a little more pressure and the rod weather-vaned in his hands. The tarpon was off.

We watched the big fish spiral to the bottom and right itself just above the turtle grass. We watched its broad dark back melt into the shadows and dreamily, majestically swim out of our lives forever. On the one hand, I felt an immediate sense of relief, but on the other hand, I despaired at the loss and how close we had come to angling immortality. There was nothing to say and nothing left of the day. We sat in our respective ends of the boat for a long time, a leaden Florida sun heavy on our shoulders. We sat in silence, reliving the moment that had shaped the longest and shortest ten minutes of our fishing lives.

The wing of a cormorant ticked the surface of the water. A Navy jet howled across the sky. The wake of a distant steamer passed under our hull. In the distance I heard the manic voice of a flats guide berating his client. A school of tarpon rolled into range. We did not get up.

LORD OF THE WINDS

Gary Soucie

Humbly do I beseech thee, o mighty King Aeolus, Lord of the Winds, that thou wouldst command Zephyr to sigh gently in the west, or Notus in the south, that I might find and catch a fish upon the flats, be it bonefish, permit, or tarpon. I shall not kill the fish I seek, nor pollute the waters upon which I navigate, so why dost thou ever send chilly-fingered Boreas out of the north against me, or Eurus howling across the long fetches of the east? What wrong have I done thee, what transgression have I committed, that thou wouldst punish me so? Forgive me, o son of the great Hippotas and husband of fair Cyane, for I know not what sin has been marked against me in the log book of the gods, and I long to make a fair cast on the flats to a fish I can see. Tantaene animis coestibus irae? I join the estimable Virgil in asking: In heavenly winds can such resentment dwell?

—a piscatorial prayer

OO FAR," THE GUIDE SAID IN EXASPERATION AS I LET another pod of bonefish get away. I stripped furiously, preparing for another cast. "Forget it," said the guide, who shall go nameless, to preserve his well-deserved reputation as a nice guy to fish with. "They're gone."

It was not the first time that day I had failed to see the bonefish in the roiled water and spooked them with a blind cast that was off the mark. "Look," the guide said, with as much patience as he could muster, "you're going to have to see them sooner and cast faster. Especially under these conditions."

Remember Joe Bfstplk, that hapless character in the Li'l Abner comics who always had a rain cloud over his head? That's me on the flats. It doesn't necessarily rain, but it always blows. And I mean always. Not balmy subtropical zephyrs, mind you. I'm talking about real wind: twenty knots or better, small-craft warnings, whole gales, that sort of thing. It never fails to blow when I'm on the flats. You could get rich betting on it.

When it comes to flats fishing, I'm downright cursed. I still haven't caught my first bonefish. Not even on spinning tackle and live shrimp. It's that bad. I've caught tarpon and permit and sharks, but never on the flats. Yes, I've caught barracuda on the flats, but who hasn't?

My failure to learn flats fishing hasn't been for want of proper teachers. Hey, I've been chased off the Lakes by squalls while fishing with Bob Trosset and Marshall Cutchin, and if there are better guides, there aren't many of them.

Like too many flats wannabes, I foolishly started without a guide. It was up on the flats behind Tavernier Key, and we did everything wrong: We were four in a light, expanded-foam boat (two too many), without a push pole, in a brisk wind. At least we had the tide right. We were letting the wind drive us across the flat as the rising waters covered it. But we couldn't see the fish before they saw us. We kept spooking schools of bones. Finally, I got a decent shot at a lone fish. Luckily, I made a perfect cast with a pink Wiggle Jig (it was back before I'd taken up the fly rod). The fish kept picking up the jig by the bucktail, without ever taking the hook in its mouth. It would drop the jig and start to turn away. I'd wiggle the jig and bounce it forward a few hops. The fish would turn and pick it up again. We kept this up until the bone was within two yards of the boat and we were all crouched down below the gunwales. Finally, the fish had had enough of this nonsense and skedaddled. It was the closest I've ever come to catching a bonefish.

Even without a punishing wind, my first forays on the flats with a fly rod were spectacularly unsuccessful. As you know, you must be able to cast quickly, accurately, far, and delicately on the flats. All on one cast. In my fly-casting experience, those are almost mutually exclusive propositions. On a good day, I could maybe put two of them together, but never all four. On a bad day I couldn't put one of them together. And I was (and still am) as prone to bad-casting days as some women are to bad-hair days.

Frantically false-casting in a vain attempt at distance, I'd spook whole flats. When I could get the distance, I'd be wide of the mark or splash the line down right on top of the fish. I'd wrap the line around the rod butt or a cleat, or stand on the so-called shooting coils. I'd hook myself in the back or send the guide diving off the poling platform with an errant cast. It was awful. As my friend Jack London would observe disgustedly, "What an idiot."

Now that I've been on the flats a time or ten, I'm better at spotting fish and

"PERMIT FLATS" *Peter Corbin*

muds, and I'm probably no longer the worst caster between Key Largo and the Dry Tortugas. Still one of the worst, maybe, but not the very worst. On a really good day, I can even put three of those casting imperatives together—if the wind would just lie down. But it never does.

The last time I was out on the flats, fishing with another nameless guide, I let boredom blow my best shot. It was a windy day, of course: fifteen to twenty knots, with higher gusts. So we headed for some small flats in the lee of some small keys. After a couple of hours of fruitless poling on flat after flat (the guide spotting fish in the choppy, colored water, and me making feckless blind casts), we decided to stake out one flat and chum it. Twenty minutes passed, thirty, an hour. For want of anything else to do, I cast to a little bonnethead shark that was grazing in our chum. You guessed it: As soon as my fly landed, four bonefish came up over the edge of the flat, headed straight for us. As I lifted the line in a splashy approximation of a backcast, the fish spooked and ran. The guide had had enough.

"Maybe the wind will settle down tomorrow," he said as he started the engine. If it did, we might even try tarpon out in the channels between the flats.

Next day, we were blown out by small-craft warnings. "I've seen snakebit fishermen in my day," the guide said, "but . . ." He let his voice trail off into the howling wind.

Don't bother contacting the publisher for my phone number. You can't find out my flats-fishing schedule so you can make other plans. I've stopped making long-range plans and reservations.

Spur-of-the-moment, that's my new approach. I figure that maybe I can catch spiteful old Aeolus when he's occupied elsewhere with his bag of winds. If not, I guess I'll just keep flailing away in the tempests until the law of averages catches up with me. It always does, doesn't it?

MY KODAK MOMENT

Corbett A. Davis, Jr.

I'VE HEARD 'EM ALL. "YOU HAVE TO PAY YOUR DUES." "JUST TO JUMP A tarpon is quite an accomplishment." "The best thing about flats fishing is the scenery. Watch the birds, rays, sharks, and turtles. That's what it's all about." "The hunt's better than the catch." "Corbett, we're only out here to have fun." "Fish are just a bonus."

I do agree with all the guides that muttered these words on those long boat rides home. I'd rather be on the flats than any other place on earth. It clears the brain. A good place to relax and concentrate at the same time. Hear what you see and see what you hear.

If Webster had ever fished the Marquesas, I wonder what his definition would be:

The flats . . . (noun) . . . skinny water with a serene, tranquil environment; lush with sea life, underwater botanical gardens, and habitat for the most elusive fish on earth.

"Okay," I thought, "I'm ready to put the scenery behind me and land a tarpon." I'd seen rays. I'd jumped tarpon and if I saw another cormorant spook one more fish, my next trip would include a 12-gauge. I was very happy with my standing at the moment. In my eyes, I'd finally paid my dues and the pressure was off. I was overdue.

I had researched the topic well. I'd read about 380 books on tarpon fishing, knew the Bimini twist and Huffnagle well enough to tie in my sleep, and had tied enough Marquesas Sunrises and Black Deaths to outfit every store in the Keys. I had practiced my casting daily. Using an 11-weight Sage and a Billy Pate tarpon reel, I could now cast 100 feet into gale force winds with only one backcast. Yeah, right! I could also leap tall buildings. It really didn't matter because we were leaving the dock the next morning at five A.M. If I couldn't cast by now, I never would.

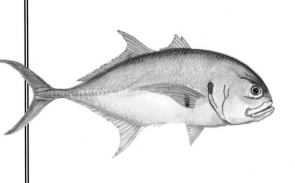

JACK CREVALLE

Caranx hippos

Casting flies for tarpon in any of the channels from the Contents to the Marquesas will often produce hookups with the jack family. They are everywhere, and if you hook a ten- or twenty-pounder you'll think you have a much larger fish on your line. Stubborn, tough and very strong, these wide-bodied fish are a game fish by any measure.

Another important factor in catching fish is having the correct attire. I'd spent years of research in collecting the perfect clothing. Nancy, my wife, had sewn up my lucky shorts one more time. Their faded orange color was stained with snapper and grouper blood left over from a time when I enjoyed killing fish. I wore those to prove to the tarpon gods that I was sorry for past behavior. Nancy never ironed these shorts; she knew it would surely remove their mystical powers. My T-shirt was a gift from Captain Fuzz Head, a good friend in Hilton Head. The fish on the front were now as hard to see as "Silva Dolla Tarpon Tournament" was to read on the back. But the good vibes were all still intact. My hat was also a gift from a good friend, Captain Awby Meador in Point Clear, Alabama. It's a Hemingway cap with a deer-skin bill long enough to shade my face from those dreaded rays. I wore no shoes. This made it easier for me to tell when I was standing on my fly line. With my amber-colored polarized glasses, I was all set. I hoped the deities who watch over that beautiful atoll of mangrove keys would look favorably upon my clothing. I wore it for them.

After a feast of fried grouper, black beans, yellow rice, flan, and a cup of con leche at Coco's Cantina on Cudjoe Key, we went home, checked our leaders and knots, tied our best fly, set the alarm, and hit the sack.

As usual, visions of jumping tarpon, huge schools of permit and twelve-pound bonefish kept me awake for about three hours. I'm sure it wasn't the Cuban coffee.

I awoke as the radio bellowed tunes that my disoriented brain did not recognize. This will be a great day, I thought.

My dad, Corbett Sr., and I were meeting our friend Jeffrey at Garrison Bight a good hour and a half before sunrise. Jeffrey is an amazing guide. Not only can he maneuver his Maverick skiff through the flats between Key West and the Marquesas, he can do it in total darkness. Jeffrey knows the tides, the channels, and the conditions like no one else. Most important, he knows where the tarpon live.

As the flickering lights of Key West disappeared behind us, we made our way across Boca Grande Channel and arrived at the Marquesas precisely at sunrise. What a sight to see. We spooked a flock of white ibis as we took a shortcut through the mangroves. They looked almost golden in the morning sun. Those wise men are right. It doesn't get much better than this. Any fish would definitely be a bonus.

Up on the bow as Jeffrey poled, I stripped out my fly line and was as ready as I would ever be. The wind was blowing about fifteen knots from the southeast and Jeffrey had spotted a couple of happy fish rolling about a hundred yards up. Before we reached them, I noticed a school of round silverfish ahead and by instinct, threw my fly into the center of the school. General hell broke loose as a thirty-pound permit sucked down my tarpon fly and headed south. All was going well until a tangled glob of knots got hung on my first running guide and snapped my leader just seconds before I would have had him on the reel.

I tied on another fly and saw the rolling tarpon that Jeffrey was stalking. We finally got within casting distance of about five large fish. They were in a picture-

WHITE IBIS

Eudocimus albus

With its long, decurved bill and prominent black tips on its wings, the adult white ibis is easily identified. And although the immature ibis is dark brown, the flocks in flight are distinctive: a wavering string of graceful, long-necked, slow-flying waterbirds with wings that catch the sunrise in their curved undersides.

perfect daisy chain, just like in the movies. I cast to the far right corner and they all disappeared. Jeffrey was yelling, "Get ready for a take. They're following it." My knees were knocking together and my heart was pounding so loud, the fish could probably hear it. I kept stripping, and five feet away from the boat, I saw two huge silver flashes as both fish refused the fly. I looked and noticed two big strands of seaweed trailing out behind my fly. The fish were gone. I sat down to relax and have a good cry.

Dad was rigged for permit with a twelve-foot leader, ten-pound tippet and what would later become known as the "crab fly from hell." My father takes a great deal of pride in his fly tying. He once watched a shrimp swim for hours before finalizing his own deadly fly creation, the Crustacean A.D. He asked Jeffrey what he thought about his still experimental crab fly. Jeffrey said, "It looks great, but can you throw it in this wind?" A determined Corbett Sr. stood ready when Jeffrey shouted, "Permit. Eleven o'clock!" Two false casts and the crab fly was lifted straight up over the boat and hovered there for a while. Fish were gone.

The next hour or so seemed a bit foggy. We saw both tarpon and permit. Somehow they seemed to escape us. I just could not understand. These were, in fact, my lucky clothes. I'll bet Nancy ironed my pants and didn't tell me.

As the sun got higher, I got back on the bow again. The weather was gorgeous: the best I'd ever seen in the Marquesas—no wind, hot, and crystal-clear water. Great for tarpon; not so great for permit.

Jeffrey positioned the boat as he spotted two rolling fish ahead. I cast out about sixty feet to eleven o'clock. Second strip, I felt a tight line and set the hook. Before I could figure out if it was a fish or a clump of weed, an enormous explosion of water and a leaping tarpon filled my vision just fifty feet out. All I could think about was my last trip with Jeffrey a year earlier. I had hooked my first tarpon on a fly and got so excited that on his fifth jump I forgot to bow, then, snap. I was determined to give this

fish one hundred percent. No dancing, singing, or jumping up and down. He jumped; I bowed. He ran; I held tight. He went left; I went right. By the time I was sure I had him figured out, he jumped again, hit the water, and right back into the air he went. Right then a small piece of grass the exact color of my fly came out of the tarpon's mouth while he was in midair. My heart quit. However, to my surprise, I still had him hooked. He made one last run and jumped a couple more times. Jeffrey was prone at the rail of the boat explaining that a fish is caught only when the guide touches the leader. Then Jeffrey grabbed the leader, and at the same moment, the fish took off again. I heard the camera click a couple of times, and Jeffrey congratulated me on a fine catch. I wasn't satisfied with that leader stuff, however. I needed picture proof! A few moments later, Jeffrey had my tarpon by the lips, and we had finally reached our Kodak moment. As we revived and released the beauty, Jeffrey informed me that my two-hundred-pound tarpon actually weighed ninety pounds. My very first tarpon brought to the boat. What a great day!

Jeffrey headed us due east to Key West. Since morning we had seen flocks of ibis, herons, egrets, frigatebirds and of course, cormorants. We'd seen permit, tarpon, bonefish, jacks, rays, snapper, and barracuda. We watched as a cormorant swam behind a big stingray and dove underneath his wings to pick up any stray fish or crustaceans he may have stirred from the coral bottom. The only thing we did not see the entire day was another boat.

LOST AT SEA

Michael Pollack

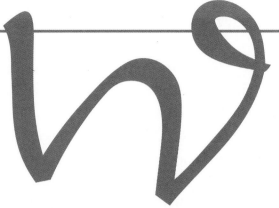

ATCHING FISHING EQUIPMENT SINK SLOWLY into the murky depths of a shark-infested channel is different from mislaying your car keys or checkbook. I am reminded daily of how important possessions and material things are to us, especially fishing equipment. The finalness one experiences as it disappears is like nothing else. I continually marvel at my ability to cope when faced with repeated equipment disasters. I have become used to such things. I am a professional fishing guide.

There have been more than a few times when some chance happening or freak mechanical failure destroyed an otherwise flawless day. Recent losses are always a major topic of conversation whenever fishing guides gather. They whine endlessly as they describe in painful detail the clear, crisp sound a graphite rod makes when it snaps or the *plooonk* of a drag washer hitting the water. The one consistency in all of it is the bewildered look on the faces of our clients. Dropping an expensive piece of equipment in the drink can be a humbling experience.

Every angler and guide has his own horror story about things he has lost or had lost for him by some unwitting soul There was the time when a "helpful" client wanted to pull up the anchor. Ever conscientious, he meticulously unhooked the clip from the boat and began hauling it up. At just that instant, a wave smacked the bow, causing him to momentarily lose his balance. Not being very coordinated or seaworthy, he let go of the line, allowing it to slip very quickly into the water. I stared in disbelief as I watched this twisted version of "hook, line, and sinker." I was out not only the line, but the chain and the anchor as well.

Some losses are not quite as expensive or as potentially dangerous as the loss of an anchor. Sometimes breaking a piece of equipment can be damned amusing, as when I fished with my buddy Eric "Break and Leave 'Em" Shores, a good friend and fellow guide. There are more anecdotes when you fish with Eric than with any other person I know. Once when we were getting ready to fish on the Bitterroot River in Montana, I broke the tip off my fly rod—a tragedy when you consider I had not even cast it one time. Eric and I went to the fly shop and I purchased my first graphite rod, state-of-the-art and expensive. We proceeded to do all the things one does to get ready for a fishing trip—visit the grocery store, stop at the gas station, drive four hours, and walk for forty-five minutes on a trail. After all the anticipation and mounting excitement, I was finally standing on the bank with my brand new rod. I strung up my new investment, building the perfect leader, and after much deliberation tied on just the right fly. My left hand on the cork handle and my right hand grasping the fly, I pulled the leader out of the rod. The nail knot on the line of my perfectly built leader caught on the tip top, and *snap* went the last six inches of my now worthless graphite rod. Eric looked at me as if I had just wet my pants. We stared at each other and then began to laugh, a laugh that started slowly and erupted into a primal howl; one would have thought it was the funniest thing either of us had ever seen. I think Eric let me take a few casts with his rod after he landed two fish. Oh well, shit happens.

At least that's what he told me on his next visit to Key West after he dropped my 1190 Sage with a #3 Fin-Nor overboard while tarpon fishing. It was about six o'clock in the afternoon on the west side of the Northwest Channel. Eric, Simon Becker, and I were into a large school of happy, rolling tarpon. We were all casting at the same time;

Simon was on the bow and I was on the gunwale moving forward to cast and then back to retrieve, working in perfect harmony. It was a beautiful thing. Eric, on the other hand, being an aggressive angler, could find no room. He opted for the poling tower. The poling tower added another four feet to his six feet, making him an impressive sight casting the entire line and carefully retrieving so as not to foul it on the outboard motor, trim tabs, and other obstacles at the stern. Well, he hooks one . . . I see the fish jump; it's about sixty pounds. The next thing I see is the rod hitting the water, the chartreuse backing stretched out on the flat-calm surface. The fish jumps again, then in what seemed like slow motion, I see Eric flying through the air, sprawled in a half jump, half belly flop desperately attempting to reach the rod. Too late, I had already made my own move. In that split second when I saw the rod go, I dropped my rod in the boat and lunged after the disappearing one.

I surfaced to see Eric frantically swimming in the direction of where the fish had last jumped. Simon was in a fit of manic laughter, I was spewing sea water, and Eric, well, he had that look on his face. The fish must have spit the hook because we never saw it jump again. We never saw the rod again, either.

Because of their size, tarpon are probably the most formidable and physically challenging fish of the flats and the most ruinous when it comes to equipment. But hooking up with a tarpon is like an addiction; you can never get enough. My good friend John can attest to that. When it comes to trashing equipment, I have to admit I am right up there at the top of the list.

John and Jean Cole and I left the dock at six A.M. In the still calm of predawn there was just barely enough gray light to find our way. Headed toward Man-o-War Harbor, the water was smooth as the skiff loped along in a way that made the water seem soft. Birds were flying around us and low over the water. I brought the boat off

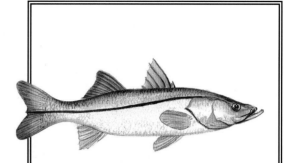

SNOOK
Centropomus undecimalis

One of the top ten on any fly caster's list of warm-water game fish, snook are tropical creatures and find Lower Keys waters to their liking. These long-snouted, silver fish with an unmistakable dark stripe from gills to tail will strike like a rocket when they're hungry; when they're not, you might as well cast to a buoy.

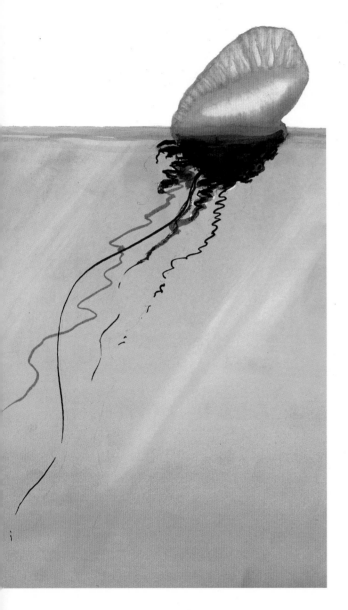

PORTUGUESE MAN-OF-WAR

Physalia pelagica

After several days of southerly breezes, the translucent, crested, pale blue membranes that are the man-of-war's inflated float show up here and there on the surface. Below are long tentacles that will give a toxic sting even after they break from the float. It is the most powerful sting of any marine organism. Do not touch!

plane and shut off the engine just past the flashing red channel marker. The tide was still incoming and carried the boat into the basin. We immediately saw a tarpon roll, its silver side exposed briefly. As it grew lighter, there were more tarpon rolling in casting range. We were in them thick; you could cut the excitement. I lowered the anchor off the stern in about thirty feet of water. One rolled just in front of the boat. John made about three casts, and *bang!* The line went so tight, water shot off it in a slow-motion dance that lasted a split second. The tarpon jumped and spit the hook. The fish was about a hundred pounds. It always happens that fast: a split moment that lasts in mind's eyes a lifetime. John hands me the rod. A couple of casts and I have one on, but my tarpon just sits there and does not run or jump.

I keep hitting him with the rod tip setting the hook . . . jab, jab, jab. I look at the line on the deck before it clears the reel. What I see is a tangled mess the size of my fist; it is definitely not going to pass through the guides. At this moment my tarpon decides to run and makes a spectacular jump. The fish is clearly hooked and makes another burning run. I point the rod right at the fish, thinking the line will hit the stripping guide and break me off. The knot does go through the guides on the butt section but catches on the first guide of the rod's tip section. I think about breaking the fish off . . . too late. The rod tip has separated from the butt section and is sliding down the line. The rod tip slips out of sight into the dark water, but the knot is there for all to see. Everyone is laughing hysterically. I pull up and reel down on the fish until the knot is close enough to grab. I hand the rod to John and desperately try to untie the tangled mess. With only a few loops to go, the tarpon makes another great run, taking the leader around a crab trap line a hundred feet to port. The line goes slack. I heard Davy Jones was opening a fly shop.

Rods and reels are probably the most common things to be lost or broken. But what about those uncommon things, like cotter pins? I was running my skiff around Lavina Bank toward the ocean when I picked up some weeds on my prop. No big deal. I brought the boat off plane at the sound of the overheat alarm, putting the engine in reverse to spin the weeds loose from the propeller. When it seemed the weeds were clear, I put the throttle forward. Nothing happened, just the loud rev of the outboard. The engine whined, but the boat lay still in the water. I trimmed up the motor; my heart sank when I realized the propeller was gone. Everything was gone— propeller, washers, nut, and the little insignificant cotter pin. I was looking at a barren shaft. Alone, on the edge of Boca Grande Channel, late in the afternoon, thirteen miles from Key West, fearing the boat would be swept from the protection of the flats out into the big water, I did what any well-trained captain would do . . . PANIC!

Adrenaline and sweat flowing like the outgoing tide saved me from certain doom. Racing around the boat, I was able to anchor but failed repeatedly to raise anyone on the nonfunctioning VHF radio. Then, out of nowhere, bearing directly toward me from the west, my good friend Jeffrey Cardenas came to my rescue—the cavalry had arrived, like an avenging angel sent by the propeller gods to deliver me safely to the dock.

The guy in the parts department at the marina told me, "Never heard of such a thing. Fifteen years in parts and I never heard of nobody break a pin like that." Somehow, it was not that reassuring.

Like a hammer to a carpenter or a scalpel to a surgeon, the push pole is to the flats guide. To break one is frustrating; to lose one is traumatic.

It was one of those mornings that are completely overcast and threatening. A storm front with high winds and rain was moving east from the Dry Tortugas at twenty-five miles per hour. After some scientific calculations, I concluded that there was a window of opportunity to save half the day. Fishing for jack crevalles seemed like a logical choice. My client, Jake Hicks, being the adventurous sort, was ready to go. Once out in the channel west of Cottrell Key we looked for some top water action. Popping bugs are truly spectacular when the jacks come up to the surface and rush the fly with their little buddies all pushing and shoving each other trying to grab what they think is food. The jacks thrashed, spray flying, then disappeared, followed by an eighty-pound bull shark, dark in color, graceful, and surprisingly swift. That morning we lost several popping bugs and three jacks to sharks. Not a game if you are a jack, or overboard. It soon became clear to us that we were not long on the water. The weather was a constant topic of conversation and speculation. We watched the ominous squall line approaching as the wind increased. The first bolt of lightning crossed the sky, and we about fell over each other getting the rods stored and the engine down and started. We roared off into the menacing wind shift and cooling temperature. The tide was too low to jump over the flat on the backside of Cottrell, an obvious shortcut that would have saved us from traveling around the long reef of hard coral on the Gulf side. The wind was now blowing thirty-plus knots, and the waves seemed huge. Jake and I were getting soaked by the spray. Every time the boat came off one wave, it slammed into the next. Water exploded, soaking us to the bone. The slam and pound, spray and drench routine continued with following seas most of the six miles back to the dock. I finally pulled safely into my boat slip. Jake turned to me and said, "Mike, where's your push pole?"

The thirty-two-ounce, $531.57 graphite push pole used to maneuver my small skiff through the shallow waters of the flats was gone forever, lost at sea, yet another casualty.

The fish that push pole and I had seen, the days we had spent together. It was like losing my best friend. For the next three days I would stand on the dock staring forlornly out to sea. I lay awake at night imagining my push pole being jettisoned into the big waves of the Atlantic like so much flotsam. I ran the scenarios over and over in my head. I questioned local captains about their knowledge of directions and drift. Rick Dostal of Waterfront Baits and Tackle suggested that perhaps I should seek out some psychiatric therapy. I opted to purchase a new push pole, perhaps with a lanyard.

I really do not get sentimental about things I have lost. What would be the point? After all, who has the time when you are constantly replacing gear?

FIRST CASTS

Rip Cunningham

IKE MANY SPORTS WITH DEDICATED, BORDERING ON WACKO, enthusiasts, fishing is ripe with clichés. Things like: the big one that got away, big as a horse, that one has shoulders, strong as goat's breath or one last cast.

And with the hundreds of boats whose name include "last cast," there seems to be a strong emphasis on the ending process. However, it is the beginning that I find important, since anticipation usually outshines actuality.

It is only by sheer irony that Key West plays any part in this, but irony, like the Lord, moves in silent and mysterious ways. Since I have been thinking more and more about this subject, I am beginning to build a personal superstition, "God, not on the first cast."

Now, of course, I have to explain the rules of the game. There are first casts and there are first casts. I'm not talking about first casts into a school of sixteen-pound bluefish bent on consuming anything that moves or doesn't move in the ocean. Heck, if you don't catch one on your first cast, then you should quietly stow your tackle and fade into the setting or rising sun. I'm talking about those plain vanilla days, when the odds are not necessarily in your favor. Like a day not long ago when my son and I arrived at a favorite small lake hoping for a heavy mayfly hatch and rising trout. We found gusting southwest wind and no sensible bugs to be seen. Not to worry, my son's first cast produced a five-pound rainbow. Those are the days and the first casts. Don't ask what happened next.

It was my first trip to Key West, now some twenty years in the rearview mirror. I

Peter Corbin
1993

was a neophyte staffer at *SaltWater Sportsman* and trying to appear that I knew what the hell I was doing. Although I had taken a number of tarpon and was fairly adept with a fly rod, I had never put the two together. In fact, I had never experienced the knee-jellying, brain-to-oatmeal-mush effect of seeing a tarpon coming across the flats. It is an experience that changes lives, sometimes not for the better.

My father and I were fishing with Gil Drake and on the first morning's run to the Marquesas, I was bubbling with enthusiasm, a.k.a. confidence. It seemed that I would not be disappointed. As we poled into the lagoon, a few tarpon showed in that slow, happy roll that we all love to see. I drew the short straw and my father was up first. When you fish with a true fanatic, the waiting time is divided into thirty-minute segments. Kept by an old half-hour, wind-up cooking timer, these regimented increments are only changed by hook-ups or missed strikes.

After several presentations, a tarpon rolled up, flared his gills and the battle was joined. How easy that looked, my mind told me, forgetting all the years my father had presented flies to tarpon. After the requisite crashing aerial display, the grunt-and-groan process brought the fish alongside for release.

Okay, it was now show time. Gil, being a gracious guide, handed me a brand-new custom-made by J. Lee Cuddy graphite rod and hinted that serious bodily harm would come to anyone who treated it badly. Hmm, it felt great in my hands. With unabridged enthusiasm, I stripped too much line onto the deck and began false casting to test the rod and to get my line stripped back on the deck properly. I laid a fairly long cast, but not enough to clear all the loops. As I reached down to untangle the remaining loops, I heard a stuttering, "P . . ., P . . ." from the poling platform. Simultaneously, the rod tip jerked down and the pile of line headed toward the stripping guide.

I had no idea what had grabbed the fly. It didn't jump. All I could think of was having every guide stripped off the new rod or, worse, having the tip section disappear over the horizon complete with fly line. I pointed the rod at the fleeing fish and

"THE STARTING GATE" *Peter Corbin*

extended my arm in an unanswered supplication that the fish would turn. As luck would have it, the leader parted and the only damage was to my ego. But things got worse.

Gil jumped off the poling platform exclaiming, "Did you see the size of that permit?" No, I had not even seen the permit at all. I was too busy controlling damage. To add insult, I had never caught a permit, let alone hooked one on a fly, and to this day I have yet to land one on a fly rod. Superstition or just plain fate? For the remainder of that week, I could not place a single fly correctly and never so much as pricked a tarpon. Every time the timer tolled, it tolled for me.

It was almost twenty years later that I returned to fish with Gil in Key West. I had fished the area any number of times in the interim, but not with Gil. This time, it was more of a demand performance for both of us, as we were trying to film an episode for our television series. Fishing tarpon on the flats is problematic, even when everything goes right. If you have to do it early in April with the lens of a Betacam eighteen inches from your nose all day, it's near impossible, but that's okay: The impossible just takes a little longer.

If there is any one thing that most fishermen hate, it is wind. Waking up on the first day of a TV shoot and being hateful is never a good sign. If the wind is blowing a steady twenty-five from the southeast and gusting higher, then hateful does not say enough. Pessimism starts to creep in.

A camera crew that has not filmed the flats before is oblivious to the negative conditions. I thought that we would scrub the day's shoot and then have to explain why. But no! Gil thought we should give it a try and maybe we could find a fish in the channels. "God," I thought, "the fish better not be upwind."

On those days when the foam lines are making up long and white, you are not filled with anticipation, but the show must go on. Settling in on the first flat, we loosened up for the camera with a lot of small talk and a story about a neighbor of mine

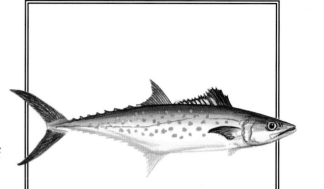

SPANISH MACKEREL

Scomberomorus maculatus

Streamlined, silver, iridescent, marked with gleaming bronze spots, this movie-star-handsome fish has more than just a beautiful body: It's a fine fighter and will eat a fly almost anytime. When they feed in the channels, cast into the white water. Excitement is guaranteed as long as they stay on top.

and his first trip to Key West. He's a sometime fisherman who basically fly-fished for trout. He had heard about tarpon on a fly and decided to give it a try. Can you believe, his first trip to Key West on his first day out and his first cast to "lollygagging and sunning" tarpon, he hooked and landed a tarpon. If I had been him, I'd have dropped everything and gone to buy a Lotto ticket. When that happens, the response about fly-fishing tarpon is forever "ho hum."

As I finished the story, we approached the channel along the flat. Yes, I saw the tarpon roll and so did Gil. The cast was across the wind. Long, but not impossible. The line shot out, almost picture book perfect. One strip and *bam!* the impossible just happened, and to make it even more unbelievable, the number one cameraman caught the whole thing on film.

It wasn't until we had filmed this one poor tarpon ad nauseam and released the worn-down fish that the euphoria of getting "something in the can" wore off and I realized what happened. It was the old first cast thing. For the remainder of the day, the jinx played true, no hits, no pricks, no rolls. The first cast in Key West had struck again.

There is no scientific basis for the phenomenon. It is not my nature to be superstitious and I have tried not to believe. Then I thought that maybe it was just me. However, remember that five-pound rainbow my son caught. That was it for the day, yet I caught a number of fish using the same kinds of flies. Perhaps it is a genetic defect. I'll have to remember to ask my father.

Good fishermen always think that the cast they are about to make is the one that will produce. If not, why make it in the first place? Now, I continue to anticipate catching on all those casts, between the first and the last. I hold my breath on the first effort and have come to realize that if I am unlucky enough to connect on the first cast, I can always make it the last and thus beat the superstition altogether.

Coral Reefs: Beautiful, Alive, Fragile, and Endangered

DeeVon Quirolo

CORAL REEFS ARE ALIVE WITH HUNDREDS OF SPECIES OF FISH, stony and soft corals, sponges, jellyfish, anemones, snails crabs, lobsters, rays, sea turtles and other sea life. This diversity of life makes coral reefs the most biologically diverse marine ecosystems on earth, rivaled only by the tropical rain forest on land.

Florida's coral reef is the only living coral barrier in North America and the third longest barrier reef in the world. These reefs are very shallow—typically only fifteen to thirty feet deep. Some reefs break the surface of the water at low tide. The barrier reef starts south of Miami and parallels the Florida Keys, lying about six miles offshore and extending southwest to the Dry Tortugas, about sixty-seven miles west of Key West.

The Florida reef tract, composed of outer reefs and patch reefs, contains more than thirty-five species of corals—over eighty percent of all coral reef species in the tropical western Atlantic—and more than 150 species of tropical fish. Corals are divided into two basic types: hard and soft. Typical hard corals found at local reefs are giant brain coral, butterprint brain coral, elkhorn, staghorn, lettuce coral, mountainous star coral, pillar coral, and leafy stinging (or fire) coral.

Soft corals found in the Keys include purple sea fans and gorgonians, such as sea plumes and sea whips. Sponges are found at all depths and filter several hundred

LOGGERHEAD

Caretta caretta caretta

Even though it's been hunted for a century, the Loggerhead is the most common sea turtle in the Lower Keys. Its nests of one hundred or more eggs have been found in the Marquesas and other sand beaches west of Key West. Weighing up to five hundred pounds, the loggerhead has made something of a comeback in recent years.

gallons of water per day. Barrel sponges and tube sponges are common at Keys reefs. Also common are anemones, simple multicelled animals with elegant tubular, translucent branches. They are similar to corals but lack the stony structure and can move on the ocean bottom. Corals are delicate structures composed of millions of tiny soft-bodied animals called polyps. It can take years for some corals to grow one inch. Corals have grown over geologic time and have been in existence about three hundred million years. A coral reef is composed of thin plates, layers of calcium carbonate secreted over thousands of years by billions of coral polyps. The reef is constantly growing new colonies of polyps on top of the skeletons of older ones. Various algaes at the reef coat the surface of the corals; they contribute to the production of calcium carbonate, the building material that makes up the calcareous exoskeleton of coral formations.

Each coral polyp resembles a tiny sea anemone and contains within its body tissues minute algae known as zooxanthellae. This algae has a symbiotic relationship with the polyp. It takes in carbon dioxide and wastes produced by the polyps, processes it through photosynthesis, and gives off oxygen and organic compounds, which are then used by the host polyp.

When adverse conditions stress the zooxanthellae, they can expel themselves from the host coral. This occurs during incidents of coral bleaching and is responsible for the loss of color in corals. The coral can recover if the stress is short-lived and the zooxanthellae return to the host coral. Many coralheads affected by coral bleaching in the Keys and the Caribbean are not recovering, indicating that the conditions have not allowed the symbiotic algae to survive in local waters. These stresses could include increased sea temperatures, elevated salinity levels, or elevated ultraviolet light levels.

The coral polyp is a hollow, cylindrical animal with a mouth surrounded by tentacles. The stinging cells of the polyp capture plankton for food. During the day, the tentacles are folded into the digestive sac of the polyp. At night, when the tentacles are extended, the coral reef is an entirely different seascape, thus the popularity of night diving. During the annual coral spawning event, some polyps expel mucus carrying sperm to unite with the eggs expelled by other polyps. Once fertilized, the egg settles onto a fixed spot and "recruits" or initiates new coral growth, although it may simply provide a meal for another form of marine life or fail to recruit because of other factors.

Once the coral polyps have colonized and created a living formation, they are susceptible to damage from any source of pollution that reduces the clear, clean, nutrientfree waters required for healthy coral growth. The physical impact of boaters, divers, and snorkelers who anchor, stand, touch, or drag equipment over the fragile coral colonies is a source of much damage to coral reefs in the Keys. The nick of a diver's fin can give diseases a toehold that results in the loss of a coralhead that has grown for years. Outright loss of habitat occurs when boats accidentally run aground or tear up shallow sea grasses and tropical fish and live rock are harvested for the aquarium trade. Live rock is the rubble area of the reef that provides a nursery and breeding habitat for many reef creatures, which is why it is so valued for artificial habitats.

We can all do our part to help save the reef by avoiding all contact with the ocean bottom and by not releasing any bilge or wastewater, gear, or trash into the ocean; take your trash back to shore and recycle it.

FEAR OF THE FLATS

Whitney Griswold

HERE'S NO SEPARATING KEY WEST FLATS FISHING FROM KEY West itself. Unless you can copter into the Marquesas and get yourself lowered into a skiff, you'll have to come to some sort of reckoning with Key West first. And if you could make yourself materialize in the skiff over the town on the way, you'd miss a vital part of Key West fishing.

It's a stretch to say that fear kept me clear of Key West for years, but it's not entirely untrue. Why else would I avoid a place surrounded by fishing that seemed tailor-made for me? I love to cast, I love to look, I love silence, I love calm water, I hate diesel fumes. But if the land that the dock's attached to gives you the willies, how're you going to get out on the water?

I first decided to shun Key West twenty-five years ago. I barely knew about the great fishing there, and I was happy chasing the same old species during the same old six-month season along the northeastern coast. But I had chosen Key West as a symbol of what I thought I should avoid—a sleepy backwater where aimlessness, hiding out, and probably drinking might become chronic.

So I adopted Key West as a metaphor for the last, worst place I could imagine, a place that could come to ruin me. Key West? No thanks. A place with such a magnetic and mysterious name was not for me. As a resident of another island that had hypnotic powers at the time, I was aware and wary of what a powerful place could do to me.

So what I said, to myself and anyone I trusted not to laugh out loud, was, "I don't want to end up at fifty, down and out in Key West, living out some macho

fishing fantasy because it's the only thing I know how to do." Too glib? Sure, but it's remained a useful buoy along my way.

Finally, long after I stopped being spooked by stories of friends who'd fled there and bled there, I let myself out of my past and into Key West in my forty-ninth year. I could no longer cast all day without complaints from cranky joints the following day, but there were benefits, too: I no longer felt obligated to jam into cramped joints late at night, for example. My wife, who was with me, was better company anyway.

It was the dead of February. I was told there might be a few tarpon in the harbor, that maybe I'd have a shot at a permit, and that I could count on some action with barracuda. I knew it wasn't the best time of year, but it was the best I could do.

Even in midwinter, the flats were magical, soothing, refreshing. We fished out west, out to Boca Grande, in the backcountry up to Snipe Keys, and on the ocean side up along Saddlebunch. I caught some cuda on flies—great fun with very game fish. But mostly I watched, stared, gaped. With senses that had been dormant too long, we soaked up the sights around us as though we hadn't seen anything pretty in years. And when we came ashore in the afternoon, regenerated, we had this funny, funky town to feast on until I shut my eyes and let sleep take over, but not before I saw a low line of mangroves on the horizon, an image that my eyes had stored for one last look on the way to rest.

Two weeks later, at a fly-fishing show during a snowstorm in Boston, I was invited back to Key West in May. Wasn't the middle of May the time to be in Key West for tarpon? Well yes, the guide said, and someone had canceled on the seventeenth, eighteenth, and nineteenth—would those days work for me? I didn't bother to check my calendar. If there was a conflict, the other thing would be rescheduled, that's all.

Before the snow had melted from the playing field across from my house, I was out there casting. In March, when the weather seemed actively hostile, and in April,

"EDGE OF THE MANGROVE" *Peter Corbin*

when it was only faintly hopeful, I'd clamber over the six-foot chain link fence, after squeezing my old black fiberglass Harnell "light" fly rod through the dirt under the fence. I'd practice-cast until the loop disintegrated and the wind knots started to multiply. I made some progress, but enough to make a difference on the water, with real fish?

Four days before I was to leave for Key West, something let go in my right fore-arm midway into a backcast. The pain was so sharp that I let go of the rod. It fell limp on the cold mud behind me. Out came the heating pad, the ice, the Advil, followed by a desperate trip down the halls of doctors' offices in the hospital, where I had hoped to find an orthopedist who'd give me a shot to save my dream fly-fishing trip. No luck.

I decided not to pick up the Harnell again, to rest the arm as long as I could. But I only had three days, and the pain in my forearm felt as if it would last longer than that. Still, I hoped it might heal itself. When I finally got out there, with the crack guide and the real photographer, and there were actually rolling tarpon to throw at, it didn't take but a couple of casts to realize that it wasn't going to work.

So I watched. The guide and the photographer, who was also a fly fisherman, took turns casting and poling, and I watched. But I really wasn't missing a thing. I was getting plenty of what I really needed out there—the chance to use my eyes, the chance to focus on something other than how to move my right arm so that the rod that it held would whip a bright, limp line out to lie quietly on the surface, with the fly at its end landing a few feet in front of a tarpon.

To me, the flats are about seeing, looking, watching. I rely almost purely on my eyes out there, to spot likely spots, to aim at likely fish, to feel alive. I'd rather rely on my senses than on a machine. I like it best when the only things running are the water, maybe a few fish, and my thoughts. The latter might take a contemplative turn, if I'm out there awhile, from which I usually emerge feeling cleaner, clearer.

TURKEY VULTURE

Cathartes aura

Like so many anglers, these large, black birds with two-tone wings fly south as winter approaches. By January, they have reached the end of the line over Key West and the Marquesas and spend hours circling in large flocks high overhead, a mysterious activity called kettling.

At times the sights are overwhelming. There's so much to see above the water's surface that I may forget to look below it. Or after I've seen or felt something underwater, I can see nothing above the surface. Sometimes the looking is just too intense, and I have to refocus on the world between the gunwales, fiddling with some tackle or nibbling on a cookie.

When it feels as if the fishing is becoming secondary, I remind myself that if it weren't for the fishing, I wouldn't be out there in the first place. I'm no naturalist, nor a painter, nor a poet. I need a practical reason to be out there. It started, when I was fifteen or sixteen, with the desire to be recognized as some sort of hunter-gatherer, some sort of provider. Now fishing, its motives and rewards, are much less clear to me. But as long as the air and the water are clear, there's nothing confusing, nothing nonrenewable about just looking. The resource can handle it.

Still, as soon as I was ashore in the early afternoon of the first day of my dream trip, I headed right for a chiropractor's office I'd seen on Truman Avenue, just off Garrison Bight, on my way into town. I walked in off the street, told my story to a woman who listened and seemed intrigued. She started with some deep rubs into my forearm that both hurt and felt restorative at once and told me that the treatment would last only until I tried to cast again. I told her I'd be casting at six the next morning, and we got along fine.

Just as the sun cleared the horizon, we swung around the backside of the Marquesas, and ten minutes later I was casting—not long, not very accurately, but I was back in the game. It took just seconds to realize that active participation was every bit as important as passive observation. Who was I kidding?

I was ready for anything. Just a chance for a shot at a fish would be a triumph, considering that I couldn't cast at all the day before. With this more modest goal in mind, I relaxed. I let my instincts take over and do what my muscles couldn't. Fine, this'll work, I thought.

It would have, no doubt, but there were no fish. Third week of May, great guide, limited but effective casting skills—and there were no fish.

No fish. What do you mean, no fish? Is this a joke, or a test, or what? What kind of crazy seesaw is pumping me up and down, round and round? First, I can't cast, but I decide it doesn't matter; I'll just watch. Now I can cast a bit, and it matters plenty that there are no fish—plenty.

It may have been a test after all: Would being there be enough? The answer was immediate and unequivocal. Even with no action, being out there was a thrill, and a comfort. Salt water is elemental for me. When I'm in it or on it, I feel good, strong, grounded. Wherever I am, on the twenty-sixth floor or three hundred miles inland, I can sense the shortest route to the nearest cove, bay, or estuary. To be out on the flats, on water that's almost always calm, where it's so shallow it feels as though I could always slip over the side into my element at any time—that's when I feel most alive.

And it turns out that some of the best flats around are around a town that I loved at first sight. I know there's not much left of the wild, wide-open town that I had loved to hate for so long. I know that Duval Street might as well be a theme park, and that the whole town has become something of a caricature of itself. And I know that guiding can get to you, that there are some built-in limits that aren't apparent to an angler who's being whisked over a mirror of water at daybreak with a whole day of fishing, and possibility, ahead.

So, why is it that I have often found myself wondering how to rearrange my life so that I could spend half the year there? Now, from where I sit, strapped to a desk and fifty years old, I say to myself and anyone I can trust not to laugh out loud, "Shoot, living in Key West and spending five or six days on the water every week, it looks pretty good to me." Now, in the nineties, sleepy backwaters are sought out for privacy, regeneration, even peace. Was I ahead of my time all that time?

Holding a half-full glass, I picture a place that looks cleansing, not washed out. But I have to get out on the water, out on the flats, for the picture to come in clear, loud and clear. And when it does, I can't help but wonder: How you gonna keep me back on the beach, after I've seen Man Key?

ABOUT THE CONTRIBUTORS

Peter Kaminsky is a television producer and a newspaper columnist and has written many articles for national magazines. Fishing, however, is what he'd rather be doing most of the time.

Poet, novelist, and essayist, as the jackets of his several fine books will tell you, **Dan Gerber** is also a finely tuned flats fisher, quite in harmony with that rare environment.

Russell Chatham is an artist, a writer, and one of those fortunate few who fished the waters off Key West in those long-ago days when the flats and their fine fish were still a secret kept from most of the world.

Former flats guide, writer, photographer, fly-fishing instructor, and proprietor of The Saltwater Angler fishing headquarters in Key West, **Jeffrey Cardenas** has earned his flats-fishing doctorate.

A songwriter, musician, novelist, and angler, **Jimmy Buffett** lives in Key West much of the year and has fished the flats from the Contents to the Marquesas.

There are not many fishing writers who have been at it longer than **George Reiger,** and none with as long a list of fine fishing books with his name on the cover.

Nick Lyons has written books and articles about fishing, published books about fishing, and has landed a tarpon on a fly while fishing in the Marquesas.

Author and columnist **Calvin Trillin** is president-for-life of the Key West Anglers Club, a splendid institution that still lives in the memories of its distinguished members, and only therein.

The author of eight books and scores of articles for *Sports Illustrated*, **Robert F. Jones** fishes and writes about it with the head-on energy and exuberance of a man who loves his work.

Thomas McGuane, one of those prescient anglers who first fished Key West waters thirty years ago, wrote his first novel, *The Sporting Club,* in 1968. It was properly praised as the opening work in a long and distinguished writing career.

John Cole is still fishing and writing about it, as he has for so many years. His books include *In Maine, Striper,* and *Fishing Came First.*

JEFFREY CARDENAS

Brad Burns lives in Maine, where he is chairman of the state's chapter of the New England Coastal Conservation Commission. He finds time to fish from Labrador to Key West.

A neighbor of Gil Drake's and, like him, a flats-fishing guide, **Captain Harlan Franklin** has a zest for life and his livelihood. He is indeed a happy angler.

A charter skipper and a man who feeds giant tarpon from his Stock Island dock, **Captain Dave Harris** is an enthusiastic observer of wildlife above and below Summerland Key waters.

As a young man in Key West, **John Leslie** fished commercially, spending many long nights alone on his boat off the Marquesas. Now he spends time alone in his Summerland Key study, writing novels—five, so far.

John Graves, an award-winning writer long identified with his home state of Texas, is best known for his books *Goodbye to a River, Hardscrabble,* and *The Last Running.*

Formerly an L.L. Bean vice president and director of its fishing departments, **Brock Apfel** has fished around the world and has written for many angling publications.

Best known as an angling artist, **Peter Corbin** became a flats-fishing author immediately after he scored his first grand slam.

An exception to the rule that great writers are not recognized by their own generation, poet, novelist, and screenwriter **Jim Harrison** is also a fisherman and a legend.

If you have read only one sentence about sport fishing in any fishing publication, it was probably written by **Bernard "Lefty" Kreh.** He's been writing longer and for more different editors than anyone else out there. And he's done more fishing.

Alan Farago, now living in Miami, is one of the happy few who not only had a home and family in Key West, but also owned a fine flats skiff and used it often and with considerable success.

Novelist, naturalist, nature writer, and explorer **Peter Matthiessen** is also a fisherman and has been since his early boyhood summers on Fishers Island.

The longtime author of *The New York Times* column "Outdoors," **Nelson Bryant** lives on Martha's Vineyard, where he fishes, plans fishing trips, and continues to write for the *Times* and angling journals.

Not many south Florida guides have been fishing and guiding as long as **Captain Flip Pallot** has. Like his friend and fellow fly caster Lefty Kreh, Pallot is a charter member of the fly-fishing hall of fame.

Nathaniel P. Reed is a south Florida native who, as an under-secretary of the Department of the Interior, was the primary force working to protect the waters from the Contents to the Marquesas. He has given all of us good reason to be grateful.

An angler who once fished the flats for thirty straight days in an effort to learn the waters off Key West well enough to catch fish on a fly, **Guy de la Valdéne** has proven that lesson well worth every sacrifice.

A former editor of *Audubon* magazine, a committed fly fisher, and a fine writer whose articles appear often in national magazines, **Gary Soucie** has quested after tarpon and permit in spite of wretched weather and various catastrophes.

Just because **Corbett A. Davis, Jr.,** lives in Pensacola, where his business is, doesn't mean he can't find the time to fish the waters off Key West, which he does regularly and often.

Still a young man, **Captain Michael Pollack** is already a seasoned and skillful Key West flats guide who has his career well in hand: Montana trout in the summer, tarpon and permit all winter long.

As editor-in-chief of *Salt Water Sportsman*, **C. M. "Rip" Cunningham, Jr.,** reads a great deal of angling literature. Every now and then, he leaves his desk for a chance to live what he reads about.

DeeVon Quirolo and her husband, Craig, founded Reef Relief, the Key West-based nonprofit organization that does the most to protect the flats and their irreplaceable coral reefs.

Former managing editor of *Salt Water Sportsman*, **Whitney Griswold** helps direct the New England East Coast Conservation Association.

Artist **David Harrison Wright** lives and works in Key West when he is not sailing the waters around it.

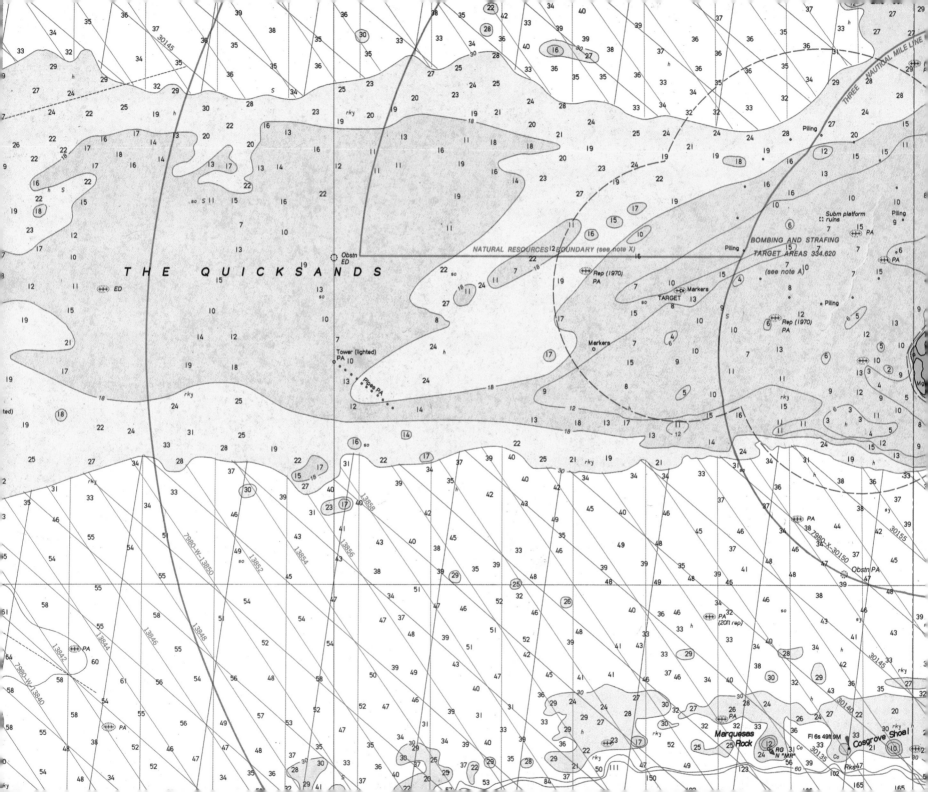